The Signature in Law

From the Thirteenth Century
to the Facsimile

OBserving Law – IALS Open Book Service for Law

The Signature in Law

From the Thirteenth Century
to the Facsimile

Stephen Mason
of the Middle Temple, barrister

Published under a CC BY-NC-ND 4.0 licence

© Stephen Mason, 2022

The author asserts his rights under the Copyright, Designs and Patents Act 1988 to be identified as the author of this work.

978-1-911507-33-8 (paperback version)
978-1-911507-31-4 (epub version)
978-1-911507-32-1 (Open Access PDF version)

Institute of Advanced Legal Studies
University of London
Charles Clore House
17 Russell Square
London
WC1B 5DR

http://ials.sas.ac.uk

	Rights in property	30
	Voting	30
	Human Fertilisation and Embryology Act 1990	30
	United States of America	31
The use of a surname		32
	Statute of Frauds	32
	Deeds	33
The use of a trade name		33
A partial signature		34
Words other than a name		35
An identifying phrase		36
Abbreviation of a name		37

6. Marks used as signatures 39

A seal imprint		39
	Wills	39
	Interest in real property	40
	Court records	43
The use of a fingerprint		44
The use of a printed name		44
	Statute of Frauds	44
	Real property	48
	Public notices	48
The use of a lithographed name		52
The use of a rubber stamp		52
	Wills	53
	Voting	54
	Judicial use	54
	Statute of Frauds	55
	Ecclesiastical use	56
	Solicitors Act 1932	56
	Administrative use	58
	United States of America	59
A stencil-pen		62

7. Mechanical signatures 64

Signature machines		64
Mechanical marks by human action		64
	Typewriting	64
	Telegram	70
	Telex	75
	Facsimile	78

8. The writing material 85

9. An incorrect signature and absence of a signature 89

Index 91

Contents

Preface		vii
Acknowledgements		viii
Table of cases		ix
Table of statutes		xxv
1.	**An introduction to the signature**	1
	Dictionary definitions	4
	The manuscript signature	4
	Statutory definition of signature	6
2.	**The functions of a signature**	8
	The primary evidential function	8
	Secondary evidential functions	9
	Cautionary function	9
	Protective function	9
	Channelling function	10
	Record-keeping function	10
3.	**Disputing a manuscript signature**	11
	Defences	11
	Evidence of the manuscript signature	11
	The identity of the person affixing the manuscript signature	12
	Intention to authenticate and adopt the document	13
4.	**Methods of authentication before manuscript signatures**	15
	Objects as a means of authentication	15
	The seal	15
	Witnesses and scribes	16
	The sign of the cross	17
	The chirograph	17
5.	**Manuscript signatures**	19
	Impression of a mark	19
	Bills of exchange	19
	An interest in real property	20
	Wills	20
	United States of America	21
	Illegible writing	22
	Assisted signature or mark	24
	Wills	25
	A name without a signature	25
	Mistake as to the name	25
	Variations of a name	26
	Voting	26
	Wills	26
	United States of America	26
	The use of initials	27
	Statute of Frauds	27
	Judicial use	28
	Wills	29

Preface

This monograph was previously the first chapter of my book *Electronic Signatures in Law*, which was first published by LexisNexis Butterworths in 2003, followed by a second edition published by Tottel in 2007, a third edition published by Cambridge University Press in 2012 and the fourth edition published by the Institute of Advanced Legal Studies for the SAS Humanities Digital Library, School of Advanced Study, University of London in 2016. Sadly, I was unable to find a lawyer or legal academic willing to join me for a further edition with a view to taking over the entire text, so the book is no longer published. Given this state of affairs, Daniel Seng and I agreed that it was appropriate to incorporate the relevant text on electronic signatures into the fifth edition of *Electronic Evidence*, giving it the new title of *Electronic Evidence and Electronic Signatures*.

The Institute of Advanced Legal Studies approved the publication of an updated version of the first chapter as a monograph. I do not claim the text to be comprehensive, although I have tried to be thorough in researching the case law. I have made great effort to ensure I cover as many common law jurisdictions as I have been able.

The purpose of discussing the case law before the widespread use of signatures in electronic form was to highlight the fact that judges have had to interpret the meaning of a signature in the light of the practical problems raised by litigants. For instance, judges have had to determine whether the use of initials constitutes a manuscript signature, or they have had to determine whether printing a name on an invoice is a signature. It is for this reason that I thought an introduction to the past will help people understand that electronic signatures are merely another form of technology that requires interpretation in the legal context.

Stephen Mason
Langford, Bedfordshire
2022

Acknowledgements

I thank everyone who has kindly helped me in researching the text of this monograph over the years, including the members of staff at the libraries of the Institute of Advanced Legal Studies and Middle Temple. I also thank the copyeditor, Lorraine Slipper, for her superb attention to detail, and to Sandy Dutczak, the IALS Digital Projects and Publications Manager at the Institute of Advanced Legal Studies, who has seen this text through the publishing process.

Naturally, I also thank my wife, Penelope, for supporting me without complaint.

Table of cases

Australia

Federal
Neill v Hewens (1953) 89 CLR 1 — 65 fn 4
Torrac Investments Pty Ltd v Australian National Airlines Commission [1985] ANZ Conv. R 82 — 78 fn 56

New South Wales
Molodysky v Vema Australia Pty Ltd (1989) NSW ConvR 55446, [1989] AUConstrLawNlr 143 — 79 fn 62

Victoria
Tina Motors Pty Ltd v Australia and New Zealand Banking Group Ltd [1977] VR 205 — 11 fn 1

Canada

Federal
R v Fredericton Housing Limited [1973] FC 196, [1973] CTC 160 — 69 fn 24
R v Kapoor 52 CCC (3d) 41 — 23 fn 27
R v Welsford, Re [1967] 2 OR 496, [1968] 1 CCC 1, 2 CRNS 5 — 55 fn 78
Schultz, Re (1984), 8 DLR (4th) 147 — 30 fn 74

British Colombia
Beatty v First Exploration Fund 1987 and Company, Limited Partnership 25 BCLR2d 377 (1988) — 84 fn 89
R v Blumes, 2002 BCPC 45 (CanLII) — 58 fn 88
R v Pearce, 2000 BCSC 0376 — 58 fn 88

New Brunswick
United Canso Oil & Gas Ltd, Re (1980) 12 BLR 130, 76 APR 282, 41 NSR (2d) 282 (TD) — 58 fn 90, 82 fn 76

Ontario
MacDonald v Sun Life Assurance Company of Canada [2006] OJ No 4428 (Sup Ct) (QL), 2006 Can LII 41699 (ON SC) — 53 fn 67
R v Burton [1970] 3 CCC 381, [1970] 2 OR 512, 8 CRNS 269 (Ont HCJ) — 55 fn 77
R v Parkinson [2002] OJ No 5478 (Ct J) (QL) — 58 fn 88

Denmark
Case U.1959.40/1H (2009) — 85 fn 3

England and Wales
Adam v Kerr (1798) 1 B & P 360, 126 ER 952 — 19 fn 4
Adams, In the Goods of (1872) LR 2 P & D 367 — 86 fn 7
Addy v Grix (1803) 8 Ves Jun 185, 32 ER 324 — 41
Allen v Bennet (1810) 3 Taunt 169, 128 ER 67 — 48 fn 42

Baker v Dening (1838) 8 AD & E 94, 112 ER 771	20 fn 10
Ball v Dunsterville (1791) 4 TR 313, 100 ER 1038	42 fn 16
Bartletts de Reya v Byrne [1983] 1WLUK 17, (1983) 133 NLJ 1101, Times, 14 January 1983, (1983) 127 SJ 69, [1983] CLY 3604	37 fn 121
Bateman v Pennington (1840) 3 MooPCC 223	85 fn 4
Behnke v Bed Shipping Co. [1927] 1 KB 649	71 fn 32
Bennett v Brumfitt (1867–68) 3 LRCP 28	54 fn 71, 63 fn 108
Blades v Lawrence (1873–74) 9 LRQB 374, (1874) 43 LJR QB 133	54 fn 73, 57 fn 87
Blay v Pollard and Morris [1930] 1 KB 628	13 fn 6
Bleakley v Smith (1840) 11 Sim 149, 59 ER 831	89 fn 3
Blewitt's Goods, Re (1879–81) 5 PD 116	30 fn 69
Borman v Lel [2001] 6 WLUK 189, [2002] WTLR 237, [2002] CLY 4329 also known as: Parsons, In the Estate of	44 fn 26
British Estate Investment Society Ltd v Jackson (H M Inspector of Taxes) (1954–58) 37 Tax Cas 79, [1956] TR 397, 35 ATC 413, 50 R & IT 33	58–59 fn 91
Brown v National Westminster Bank Ltd [1964] 2 Lloyd's Rep 187, [1964] 6 WLUK 133, [1964] CLY 191	11 fn 1
Bryce's Goods, Re (1839) 2 Curt 325, 163 ER 427	20 fn 13
Brydges (Town Clerk of Cheltenham) v Dix (1890–91) 7 TLR 215	48 fn 47
Central Motors (Birmingham) v PA & SNP Wadsworth (trading as Pensagain) [1982] 5 WLUK 265, [1983] CLY 6u, [1982] CAT 231, 28 May 1982, (1983) 133 NLJ 555	3 fn 12, 13–14 fn 10
Chalcraft's Goods, Re [1948] P 222, [1948] 1 All ER 700, 65 TLR 246, [1948] 3 WLUK 52, [1948] LJR 1111, (1948) 92 SJ 181, [1947–51] CLY 10955, also known as Chalcraft v Giles	34 fn 104
Champion v Plummer (1805) 5 Esp 239, 170 ER 798, 1 Bos & P (NR) 252, 127 ER 458	48 fn 42
Chichester v Cobb (1866) 14 LTNS 433	28 fn 56
Christian Goods, Re (1849) 2 Rob. Ecc. 110, 163 ER 1260	29 fn 68
Clark's Goods, Re (1839) 2 Curt 329, 163 ER 428	29 fn 67
Clarke's Goods, Re (1858) LJR 27 NS P & M 18, 1 Sw & Tr 592, 164 ER 611	25 fn 40
Clipper Maritime Ltd v Shirlstar Container Transport Ltd (The 'Anemone') [1987] 1 Lloyd's Rep 546, [1987] 2 WLUK 45, [1987] CLY 1846	75 fn 49
Cohen v Roche [1927] 1 KB 169, [1926] 6 WLUK 88	33 fn 100
Cooch v Goodman (1842) 2 QB 580, 114 ER 228	42 fn 17
Cook, In the Estate of, [1960] 1 WLR 353, [1960] 1 All ER 689, [1960] 2 WLUK 75, 75 ALR2d 892, (1960) 104 SJ 311, [1960] CLY 3327, also known as Murison v Cook	35 fn 111
Co-operative Bank plc v Tipper [1996] 4 All ER 366, [1995] 11 WLUK 74, Times, 5 July 1996, [1996] CLY 409	86 fn 8
Copeland v Smith [2000] 1 WLR 1371, [2000] 1 All ER 457, [1999] 10 WLUK 381, [2000] CP Rep 14, (1999) 143 SJLB 276, Times, 20 October 1999, [1999] CLY 457	28 fn 58, 59 fn 95
De Beauvais v Green (1905–06) 22 TLR 816	56 fn 80
Debtor (No 2021 of 1995) ex parte, Inland Revenue Commissioners v The Debtor, Re a; Re a Debtor (No 2022 of 1995) ex parte, Inland Revenue Commissioners v The Debtor [1996] 2 All ER 345, [1995] 11 WLUK 290, [1996] BCC 189, [1996] 1 BCLC 538, [1996] BPIR 398, [1996] CLY 3469	79 fn 65

Table of cases xi

Doe d. Phillips, Jones, and Morris v Evans and Lloyd (1833) 1 C & M 450, 149
    ER 476, (1833) LJ Ex 2 NS 179   43 fn 20
Donnelly v Broughton [1891] AC 435 PC   21 fn 15
Dormer v Thurland (1728) 2 Eq Ca Abr 663, 22 ER 557, 2 P Wms 506, 24 ER 837   39 fn 2
Douce's, Re the Goods of (1862) 2 Sw & Tr 592, 164 ER 1127   25 fn 41
Durrell v Evans (1862) 1 H & C 174, 31 LJ Ex 337, 9 Jur NS 104, 10
    WR 665, 7 LT 97, 158 ER 848 Ex Ch   47 fn 39
Dyas v Stafford [1882] 9 LR Ir 520   34 fn 102
Ellis v Smith (1754) 1 Ves Jun 11, 1 Ves Jun Supp 1, 30 ER 205, 34 ER 666   40 fn 5
English, Scottish & Australian Chartered Bank, In re [1893] 3 Ch 385   72 fn 35
Evans v Hoare [1892] 1 QB 593, (1892) 66 LTR NS 345   47 fn 38
Field's Goods, Re (1843) 3 Curt 752, 163 ER 890   20 fn 10
Finn, Re (1935) 105 LJP 36   44 fn 26
First National Securities Ltd v Jones [1978] Ch 109, [1978] 2 WLR 475,
    [1978] 2 All ER 221, [1977] 11 WLUK 24, (1977) 121 SJ 760, Times,
    9 November 1977, [1978] CLY 793   42 fn 18
Firstpost Homes Ltd v Johnson [1995] 1 WLR 1567, [1995] 4 All ER
    355, [1995] 7 WLUK 274, [1996] 1 EGLR 175, [1996] 13 EG 125,
    (1995) 92(28) LSG 30, (1995) 139 SJLB 187, [1995] NPC 135, Times,
    14 August 1995, [1996] CLY 5025   69 fn 25
Fitzpatrick v Secretary of State for the Environment and Epping Forest DC [1990]
    1 WLUK 107, [1990] 1 PLR 8, (1990) 154 LG Rev 72, [1990] CLY 4361a   59 fn 94
Geary v Physic (1826) 5 B & C 234, 108 ER 87   85 fn 1
George v Surrey (1830) 1 M & M 516, 173 ER 1243   19 fn 5
Glover's Goods (1847), Re 11 Jur 1022, 5 Notes of Cases 553   26 fn 43
Godwin v Francis (1870) LR 5 CP 295, 22 LT Rep NS 338   70 fn 31
Good Challenger Navegante SA v Metalexportimport SA (The 'Good
    Challenger') [2003] EWHC 10 (Comm), [2003] 1 Lloyd's Rep 471, [2003]
    1 WLUK 69, [2003] CLY 195, appealed [2003] EWCA Civ 1668, [2004] 1
    Lloyd's Rep 67, [2003] 11 WLUK 617, (2004) 101(2) LSG 27, Times,
    27 November 2003, [2004] CLY 373   76 fn 53
Goodman v J Eban Limited [1954] 1 QB 550, [1954] 2 WLR 581, [1954]
    1 All ER 763, [1954] 3 WLUK 22, (1954) 98 SJ 214, [1954] CLY 3173   56 fn 81
Grayson v Atkinson (1752) 2 Ves Sen 455, 28 ER 291, Ves Sen Supp 382,
    28 ER 556   40 fn 7
Harrison v Harrison (1803) 8 Ves Jun 185, 32 ER 324   20 fn 12
Henkel v Pape (1870) 6 LR Exch 7   71 fn 32
Hill v Hill [1947] 1 Ch 231, [1947] 1 All ER 54, [1946] 12 WLUK 8,
    176 LT 216, (1947) 91 SJ 55, [1947–51] CLY 5569   30 fn 75
Hindmarch v Charlton (1861) 8 HL Cas 160   20 fn 10, 34 fn 106, 35 fn 112
Holtam, Gillet, Re v Rogers (1913) 108 LT 732   20 fn 10
Hubert v Treherne (1842) 3 Man & G 743, 133 ER 1338   25 fn 39, 45 fn 33
Hucklesby v Hook (1900) 82 LT 117   48 fn 43
Jacob v Kirk (1839) 2 M & R 221, 174 ER 269   46 fn 36, 48 fn 42
Jefferies v BMI Healthcare Ltd (Human Fertilisation and Embryology)
    [2016] EWHC 2493 (Fam), [2016] 10 WLUK 243, [2017] 2 FLR 664,
    [2016] Med LR 656, [2017] CLY 1141   30 fn 80

Jenkins v Gainsford and Thring (1863) 3 Sw & Tr 93, 164 ER 1208,
 (1862–63) 11 WR 854 — 53 fn 68
Johnson v Dogson (1837) 6 LJ Ex 185, 1 Jur 739, 2 M & W 653,
 Murp & H 271, 150 ER 918 — 33 fn 99
Jones Brothers v Joyner (1900) 82 LTNS 768 — 47 fn 41
Joshua Buckton and Co (Limited) v London and North-Western Railway
 Company (1917–18) 34 TLR 119 — 46 fn 37
Knight v Crockford (1794) 1 Esp 190, 170 ER 324 — 25 fn 39
Lazarus Estates Ltd v Beasley [1956] 1 QB 702, [1956] 2 WLR 502, [1956] 1
 All ER 341, [1956] 1 WLUK 543, [1956] 100 SJ 131, [1956] CLY 7545 — 59 fn 93
Leeman v Stocks [1951] 1 Ch 941, [1951] 1 All ER 1043, [1951] 2 TLR 622,
 [1951] 4 WLUK 30, (1951) 95 SJ 368, [1947–51] CLY 10616 — 47 fn 39
Lemayne v Stanley (1681) 3 Lev. 2, 83 ER 545 — 39 fn 1
L'Estrange v F Graucob Limited [1934] 2 KB 394, [1934] 2 WLUK 22 — 13 fn 6
Lobb and Knight v Stanley (1844) 5 QB 574, 114 ER 1366,
 (1843–44) Law Times (2) 366 — 32 fn 88, 48 fn 45
Lord Lovelace's Case (c1632) W Jones 268, 82 ER 140, W Jones
 270, 82 ER 141 — 41 fn 14, 42
Lucas v James (1849) 7 Hare 410, 68 ER 170 — 85 fn 5
Luna, The Frances & Jane, The Luna, The [1920] P 22, (1919) 1 Ll L Rep 475,
 [1919] 12 WLUK 19 also known as: Frances & Jane, The v Luna, The — 13 fn 6
Maddock, In the Goods of (1874) LR 4 P & D 169 — 34 fn 108
McBlain v Cross (1872) LT 804 — 72 fn 33
McDonald v John Twiname Ld [1953] 2 QB 304, [1953] 3 WLR 347, [1953]
 2 All ER 589, [1953] 6 WLUK 103, (1953) 97 SJ 505, [1953] CLY 1758 — 55 fn 79
Morrison v Turnour (1811) 18 Ves 174, 34 ER 1204, 18 Ves Jun 175, 34 ER 284 — 33 fn 94
Morton v Copeland (1855) 16 CB 516 — 36 fn 118
Newell v Tarrant [2004] EWHC 772 (Ch), [2004] 4 WLUK 193, (2004)
 148 SJLB 509 — 30 fn 77
Parker v The South Eastern Railway Co. (1877) 2 CPD 416 — 13 fn 6
Paske v Ollat (1815) 2 Phill 323, 161 ER 1158 — 20 fn 14
J Pereira Fernandes SA v Mehta [2006] EWHC 813 (Ch), [2006] 1 WLR 1543,
 [2006] 2 All ER 891, [2006] 1 All ER (Comm) 885, [2006] 2 Lloyd's Rep
 244, [2006] 4 WLUK 182, [2006] Info TLR 203, Times, 16 May 2006,
 [2006] CLY 774, also known as Metha v J Pereira Fernandes SA — 33 fn 93
Phillimore v Barry (1808) 1 Camp 513, 170 ER 1040 — 27 fn 55
PNC Telecom plc v Thomas [2002] EWHC 2848 (Ch), [2002] 12 WLUK 537,
 [2003] BCC 202, [2004] BCLC 88, [2003] CLY 532 — 81 fn 75
Propert v Parker [1830] 1 Russ & M 625, 39 ER 240 — 33 fn 95
Pryor v Pryor (1860) LJR 29 NS P, M & A 114 — 13 fn 8
R v Avery (1852) 21 LJQB 430 — 30 fn 79
R v Cowper (Fitzroy) (1890) 24 QBD 533, [1890] 2 WLUK 7, (1890) 59
 LJKB (NS) 265 — 52 fn 64
R v Cowper (Fitzroy) (1889) 24 QBD 60, [1889] 12 WLUK 4 — 52 fn 64
R v Morais (Carlton) [1988] 3 All ER 161, [1988] 3 WLUK 82, (1988) 87
 Cr App R 9, (1988) 152 JP 355, [1988] Crim LR 459, (1988) 152 JPN
 383, [1988] CLY 654 — 28 fn 57
R v St Paul, Covent Garden Inhabitants (1844) 5 QB 671, 114 ER 1402,
 (1845) 7 QB 232, 115 ER 476 — 43 fn 22

R v Thwaites (1853) 22 LJQB 238	26 fn 42
R v Thomas Closs (1858) Crown Cases Reserved 460, Dears & Bell 460	5 fn 21
Ramsay v Love [2015] EWHC 65 (Ch), [2015] 1 WLUK 295	64 fn 2
Reddings Goods, Re (1850) 14 Jur 1052, 2 Rob Ecc 338, 163 ER 1338	26 fn 44
Ringham v Hackett [1980] 1 WLUK 323, (1980) 124 SJ 201, Times, 9 February 1980, [1980] CLY 158	3 fn 12, 13 fn 9
Rist v Hobson (1824) 1 Sim & St 543, 57 ER 215	89 fn 2
Roth (L.) and Co. (Limited) v Taysen, Townsend and Co. (1896–97) 12 TLR 211 CA	71 fn 32
Sadgrove v Bryden [1907] 1 Ch 318	71 fn 32
Sandilands, Re (1871) LR 6 CP 411	42–43 fn 19
Sarl v Bourdillon (1856) 1 CB (NS) 188, 140 ER 79	46 fn 35
Saunders v Anglia Building Society (formerly Northampton Town and County Building Society) [1971] AC 1004, [1970] 3 WLR 1078, [1970] 3 ALL ER 961, [1970] 11 WLUK 45, [1971] 22 P & CR 300, (1970) 114 SJ 885, Times, 10 November 1970, [1971] CLY 1805	12 fn 5
Saunderson v Jackson (1800) 2 Bos & Pul 238, 126 ER 1257	45 fn 32
Savory's Goods, Re (1856) 15 Jur 1042	29 fn 65
Schneider v Norris (1814) 2 M & S 237, 105 ER 388	45 fn 31, 48 fn 44
Selby v Selby (1817) 3 Mer 2, 36 ER 1	36 fn 115
Smith v Evans (1751) 1 Wils KB 313, 95 ER 636	40
Sperling, In the Goods of (1863) 3 Sw. & Tr. 273, 165 ER 1279	36 fn 119
Standard Bank London Limited v Bank of Tokyo Ltd [1995] 2 Lloyd's Rep 169, [1995] 3 WLUK 182, [1995] CLC 496, [1998] Masons CLR Rep 126, Times, 15 April 1995, [1995] CLY 397	80 fn 72
Taylor v Denning (1838) 3 Nev. & P. 228	20 fn 11
Tourret v Cripps (1879) 48 LJ Ch 567, 27 WR 706	33 fn 93, 48 fn 43
Trotter v Walker (1862) 13 CB (NS) 29, 143 ER 12	22 fn 24
Warneford v Warneford (1727) (Easter 13 Geo I) 2 Strange 764, 93 ER 834	4 fn 39, 41
Whitley, In re, Partners Callan's Case (1886) 55 LJCh (NS) 540	72 fn 34
Wilson v Beddard (1841) 12 Sim 28, 59 ER 1041	25 fn 38
Wright v Wakeford (1811) 17 Ves Jun 455, 34 ER 176	40–41 fn 12

Germany

AG Bonn Urteil vom 25.10.2001 3 C 193/01 Beweiskraft von E-Mails, JurPC Web-Dok. 332/2002	88
Bundessozialgericht, Beschluß vom 15.10.1996 – 14 BEg 9/96	82 fn 78
Bundesverfassungsgericht, Beschluß vom 19.12.1994 – 5 B 79/94	82 fn 78
GmS-OGB 1/98 2000	82

Hong Kong

Shenzhen Tian He Jian Sang Electronic Holdings Company Limited v Hong Kong Jian Sang Electronics (Group) Limited [2008] HKCFI 387, HCA 1587/2007	65 fn 4

Hungary

BDT 2001/496	82 fn 80

Ireland

Casey v Irish Intercontinental Bank Limited [1979] IR 364	48 fn 46
Emerson's Goods, Re (1882–83) 9 LR Ir Ch 443	40 fn 10, 41 fn 13
Kiernan's Goods, Re [1933] IR 222	23 fn 26
Lemon's Goods, Re (1896) 30 Ir LTR 127	40 fn 11
State v His Honour Judge P. J. Roe [1951] IR 172	55 fn 76

Japan

Fawlty & Co Ltd v Matsui Shoten K.K., Showa 33 (Wa) No.681, 10 November 1962	75 fn 48

Lithuania

UAB 'Bite Lietuva' v Communication Regulatory Authority AS14–77–06	82 fn 81

New Zealand

Bilsland v Terry [1972] NZLR 43	67 fn 18
Carruthers v Whitaker [1975] 2 NZLR 667	68 fn 20
Doughty-Pratt Group Limited v Perry Castle [1995] 2 NZLR 398 (CA)	30 fn 76
McNamee, In re (1912) 31 NZLR 1007	25 fn 41
Short v Graeme Marsh Ltd [1974] 1 NZLR 722	68 fn 19
Stuart v McInnes [1974] 1 NZLR 729	68 fn 21
TA Dellaca Ltd v PDL Industries Ltd [1992] 3 NZLR 88	68 fn 23
Van der Veeken v Watsons Farm (Pukepoto) Ltd [1974] 2 NZLR 146	68–69 fn 22

Poland

Resolution of the Polish Supreme Court I KZP 29/06	78 fn 61

Scotland

Allan and Crichton, Petitioners 1933 SLT (Sh. Ct.) 2	36 fn 117
American Express Europe Ltd v Royal Bank of Scotland plc 1989 SCLR 333, 1989 SLT 650 OH	33 fn 96
Crosbie v Wilson (1865) 3 M. 870	20 fn 9
Donald v M'Gregor 1926 SLT 103	34 fn 110
Draper v Thomason 1954 SC 136, 1954 SLT 222	26 fn 45
Gardner v Beresford's Trustees [1878] SLR 15 359	30 fn 78
Gordon v Murray (1765) Mor 16818	33 fn 97
Henderson v Watt (1893) 1 SLT 342	62 fn 107
Jollie v Lennie [2014] ScotCS CSOH_45	86 fn 9
Meek v Dunlop [1707] Mor 16806	29 fn 66, 30 fn 70
Moncrieff v Monypenny [1710] Mor 15936	34 fn 107
Pentland v Pentland's Trustees (1908) 16 SLT 480	36 fn 116
Rhodes v Peterson [1970] ScotCS CSOH_1, (1971) SC 56	37
Speirs v Speirs or Home Speirs (1879) 6 R. 1359	30 fn 70
Stirling Stuart v Stirling Crawfurd's Trustees (1885) 12 R. 610	23 fn 25, 53–54 fn 70
Traquair (Earl of) v Janet Gibson (1724) Mor 16809	33 fn 98
Whyte v Watt (1893) 21 R. 165	62 fn 107

Williamson v Williamson 1997 SC 94, 1997 SLT 1044, [1997] ScotCS
CSIH 3, 1997 GWD 9398, 1997 SCLR 561   89 fn 1

Singapore

Chua Sock Chen v Lau Wai Ming [1989] SLR 1119; reversed on appeal
[1992] 2 SLR 465   79 fn 64
Industrial & Commercial Bank Ltd v Banco Ambrosiano Veneto
SpA [2003] 1 SLR 221   81 fn 73
Masa-Katsu Japanese Restaurant Pte Ltd v Amara Hotel Properties
Pte Ltd [1999] 2 SLR 332   82 fn 77

South Africa

Akasia Finance v Da Souza, 1993 (2) SA 337 (W)   3 fn 13
Balzun v O'Hara [1964] 3 All SA 368 (T)   72 fn 36
Chisnall and Chisnall v Sturgeon and Sturgeon, 1993 (2) SA 642 (W)   20 fn 8
Ebden's Will (1885–86) Re, 4 Juta 495   30 fn 73
Fulton v Kee [1961] NI 1, CA (NI)   24 fn 35
Hanse v Jordan and Fuchs, 1909 19 CTR 530   20 fn 6
Hersch v Nel, 1948 (3) SA 686 (AD)   72 fn 36
Luttig v Jacobs, 1951 (4) SA 563 (OPD)   72 fn 36
Matanda v Rex, 1923 AD 435 (B)   24 fn 34
Putter v Provincial Insurance Co. Ltd, 1963 (3) SA 145 (W)   44 fn 27
SAI Investments v Vander Schyff, NO 1999 (3) SA 340 (N)   24 fn 32
Trollip, Re, 1895 12 SC 243   30 fn 71
Van der Merwe v Kenkes (Edms), BPK 1983 (3) SA 909 (T)   24 fn 33
Van Niekerk v Smit, 1952 (3) SA 17 (T)   24 fn 31
Van Vuuren v Van Vuuren (1855) 2 Searle 116   3 fn 15

United States of America

Federal

Apex Oil Company v Vanguard Oil & Services Co., 760 F.2d 417 (1985)   78 fn 58
Associated Hardware Supply Co. v The Big Wheel Distributing Co.,
355 F.2d 114 (1966)   51 fn 60
Barber & Ross Co. v Lifetime Doors, Inc., 810 F.2d 1276 (4th Cir. 1987),
3 UCC Rep.Serv.2d (CBC) 41   22 fn 21
Benedict, Trustee in Bankruptcy of Lillian E. Hargrove d/b/a Hargrove
Typesetting Services v Lebowitz, 346 F.2d 120 (1965)   66 fn 7, 67 fn 11
Bibb v Allen, 149 U.S. 481, 13 S.Ct. 950, 37 L.Ed. 819, 50 L.R.A. 240 (1893)   22 fn 21
Biegeleisen v Ross, 158 F.3d 59 (2nd Cir. 1998)   60 fn 97
Bufkin Brothers, Inc., In the Matter of, 757 F.2d 1573 (1985)   67 fn 14
Calaway v Admiral Credit Corporation, 407 F.2d 518 (1969)   67 fn 14
Excel Stores Inc., In the Matter of, 341 F.2d 961 (1965)   26 fn 48
George A. Ohl & Co. v A. L. Smith Iron Works, 288 U.S. 170, 53 S.Ct.
340, 77 L.Ed. 681 (1933)   28 fn 60
Gilmore v Lujan, 947 F.2d 1409 (9th Cir. 1991)   82 fn 83
Gilmore, W. H., 41 IBLA 25 (1979)   82 fn 83

Hill, In re 437 B.R. 503 (Bankr. W.D. Pa. 2010) — 56 fn 82
Hill v United States, 288 F. 192 (1923) — 49 fn 50
Interocean Shipping Company v National Shipping and Training Corporation, 523 F.2d 527 (1975) — 78 fn 57
Jones v Fox Film Corporation, 68 F.2d 116 (1934) — 31 fn 83
Kinney v United States Fidelity & Guaranty Company, 222 U.S. 283, 32 S.Ct. 101, 56 L.Ed. 200 (1911) — 28 fn 59, 29 fn 62
Mitchell v Mills, 264 S.E.2d 749 (1954) — 20 fn 7
Monetti S.P.A. v Anchor Hocking Corporation, 931 F.2d 1178 (7th Cir. 1991) — 31 fn 83, 51 fn 60
National Accident Society v Spiro, 78 F. 774, 24 C.C.A. 334 (1897) — 60 fn 100
Origet v United States, 125 U.S. 240, 8 S.Ct. 846, 31 L.Ed. 743 (1888) — 28 fn 59
Roberts v Johnson, 212 F.2d 672 (1954) — 65 fn 4
Salmon Falls Manufacturing Company, the v Goddard, 55 U.S. 446, 14 How. 446, 1852 WL 6760 (U.S. Mass. 1852), 14 L.Ed. 493 — 31 fn 83
Save-On-Carpets of Arizona, Inc., In the Matter of, 545 F.2d 1239 (1976) — 66 fn 10
United States of America v Juarez, 549 F.2d 1113 (1977) — 60 fn 103
Williams, Jack, 91 IBLA 355 (1986) — 83 fn 84
Vess Beverages, Inc. v The Paddington Corporation, 941 F.2d 651 (8th Cir. 1991) — 31 fn 87
Zacharie v Franklin, 37 U.S. 151, 12 Pet. 151, 1838 WL 3945 (U.S. La.), 9 L.Ed. 1035 (1838) — 21 fn 16

Alabama
Dew v Garner, 7 Port. 503, 1838 WL 1335 (Ala.) — 23 fn 28
McMillan, Ltd v Warrior Drilling and Engineering Company, Inc., 512 So.2d 14 (Ala. 1986) — 73 fn 41

Alaska
A & G Construction Co., Inc. v Reid Brothers Logging Co., Inc., 547 P.2d 1207 (1976) — 66 fn 10

Arizona
Bishop v Norell d/b/a Al Norell Company Realtors, 88 Ariz. 148, 353 P.2d 1022 (1960) — 50 fn 59
Maricopa County v Osborn, 60 Ariz. 290, 136 P.2d 270 (1943) — 60 fn 110

Arkansas
Arendt v Arendt, 80 Ark. 204, 96 S.W. 982 (1906) — 35 fn 113
Boone v Boone, 114 Ark. 69, 169 S.W. 779 (1914) — 35 fn 113
Cartwright v Cartwright, 158 Ark. 278, 250 S.W. 11 (1923) — 35 fn 113
Lee v Vaughan Seed Store, 101 Ark 68 (1911), 141 S.W. 496, 37 L.R.A.N.S. 352 — 50 fn 55
Walker v Emrich, 212 Ark. 598, 206 S.W.2d 769 (1947) — 26 fn 46

California
Berdan v Berdan, 103 P.2d 622 (1940) — 35–36 fn 114
Brewer v Horst and Lachmund Company, 127 Cal. 643, 60 P. 418, 50 L.R.A. 240 (1900) — 73 fn 41
Button's Estate, In re, 277 P. 758 reversed 287 P. 964 (1930) — 36 fn 113

Felt v L. B. Frederick Co., Inc., 92 Cal.App.2d 157, 206 P.2d 676 (1949) 51 fn 62
Hancock v Bowman, 49 Cal. 413, 1874 WL 1548 (Cal.) 49 fn 54
Henderson's Estate, In re, 196 Cal. 623, 239 P. 938 (1923) 35 fn 113
Hewel v Hogin, 3 Cal.App. 248, 84 P. 1002 (1906) 52 fn 65
Joseph Denunzio Fruit Co. v Crane, 79 F.Supp. 117, reversed on other grounds upon rehearing 89 F.Supp. 962 (1948) 78 fn 60
Ligare v California Southern Railroad Company, 76 Cal. 610, 18 P. 777 (1888) 49 fn 54
Little v Union Oil Company of California, 73 Cal.App. 612, 238 P. 1066 (1911) 65–66 fn 6
McNear v Petroleum Export Corporation, 280 P.R.Cal. 684 (1929) 74 fn 46
Marks v Walter G. McCarty Corporation, 33 Cal.2d 814 (Cal. 1949), 205 P.2d 1025 50 fn 55, 51 fn 63
Middleton v Findla, 25 Cal. 76, 1864 WL 629 (Cal.) 27 fn 50
Moore's Estate, 92 Cal.App.2d 120, 206 P.2d 413 (1949) 65 fn 4, 67 fn 17
Pennington v Baehr, 48 Cal. 565, 1874 WL 1399 (Cal.) (1874) 49 fn 52
Smith v Ostly, 53 Cal.2d 262, 1 Cal.Rptr 340, 347 P.2d 684 (1959) 49 fn 54
Weiner v Mullaney, 59 Cal.App.2d 620, 140 P.2d 704 (1943) 31 fn 84
Williams v McDonald, 58 Cal. 527, 8 P.C.L.J. 23, 58 Cal. 527, 1881 WL 1946 (Cal.) 49 fn 52

Colorado
Colorado Mercantile Co., Re, 299 F.Supp. 55 (1969) 60 fn 99

Connecticut
Bengston, Re, 1965 WL 8262 (Bankr.D.Conn.), 3UCC Rep.Serv. 283 60 fn 99
Deep River National Bank, Re, 73 Conn. 341, 47 A. 675 (1900) 60 fn 99
Horvath, Re, 1963 WL 8592 (Bankr.D.Conn.), 1 UCC Rep.Serv. 624 67 fn 14
Merrill Lynch, Pierce, Fenner & Smith, Inc. v Cole, 189 Conn. 518, 457 A.2d 656 (Conn. 1983) 51 fn 60

District of Columbia
McGrady v Munsey Trust Co., 32 A.2d 106 (1943) 62 fn 105
United States v Thompson, 2 Cranch C.C. 409, 28 F. Cas. 89, 2 D.C. 409, No 16484 (1823) 87 fn 14

Florida
Ashland Oil, Inc. v Pickard, Fla., 269 So.2d 714 (1972) 66 fn 10, 73 fn 43
Heffernan v Keith, Fla., 127 So.2d 903 (1961) 73 fn 41
Meek v Briggs, 80 Fla. 487, 86 So. 271 (1920) 73 fn 38
State v City of Fort Lauderdale, 149 Fla. 177, 5 So.2d 263 (1941) 60 fn 100
State of Florida v Hickman, Fla., 189 So.2d 254 (1966) 61 fn 104

Georgia
Bell Bros. v Western & A. R. Co., 125 Ga. 510, 54 S.E. 532 (1906) 61 fn 102
Evans Implement Company v Thomas Industries, Inc., 117 Ga.App. 279, 160 S.E.2d 462 (Ga. Ct. App. 1968) 50–51 fn 59
Evans v Moore, 131 Ga.App. 169, 205 S.E.2d 507 (1974) 51 fn 60
Horton v Murden, 117 Ga. 72, 43 S.E. 786 (1903) 21 fn 17

Kohlmeyer & Company v Bowen, 126 Ga.App. 700, 192 S.E.2d 400 (1972)   50–51 fn 59
Peoples Bank of Bartow County v Northwest Georgia Bank, 139 Ga.App. 264, 228 S.E.2d 181 (1976)   67 fn 14
Thurmond v Spoon, 125 Ga.App. 811, 189 S.E.2d 92 (1972)   21 fn 18
Troutt v Nash AMC/Jeep, Inc., 157 Ga.App. 399, 278 S.E.2d 54 (1981)   51 fn 60

Idaho
Paloukos v Intermountain Chevrolet Company, 99 Idaho 740 (1978), 588 P.2d 939, 25 UCC Rep.Serv. 655   50–51 fn 59

Illinois
Automotive Spares Corp. v Archer Bearings Company, 382 F.Supp. 513 (1974)   51 fn 60
Bogue v Sizemore, 241 Ill.App.3d 250, 608 N.E.2d 1246 (Ill.App.4th Dist. 1993)   83 fn 87
Cunningham v Hallyburton, 342 Ill. 442, 174 N.E. 420 (1930)   22 fn 23
Deskovic's Estate, Re, 21 Ill.App. 2d 209, 157 N.E.2d 769, 72 A.L.R.2d 1261 (1st Dist. 1959)   21 fn 20
Just Pants, an Illinois limited partnership v Wagner, 617 N.E.2d 246 (Ill.App. 1 Dist. 1993)   66 fn 8
People of the State of Illinois v Stephens, 297 N.E.2d 224 (1973)   61 fn 104
Prairie State Grain and Elevator Company v Wrede, 217 Ill.App. 407 (1920)   50–51 fn 59
Robertson v Robertson, 462 N.E.2d 712 (Ill.App. 5 Dist. 1984)   29 fn 63
Streff v Colteaux, 64 Ill.App. 179, 1896 WL 2352 (Ill.App. 1 Dist.)   61 fn 104
Westerman's Will, Re, 401 Ill. 489, 82 N.E.2d 474 (1948)   22 fn 23
Weston v Myers, 33 Ill. 424, 1864 WL 2948 (Ill.)   50 fn 57

Indiana
Ardery v Smith, 35 Ind.App. 94, 73 N.E. 840 (1905)   65 fn 3
City of Gary v Russell, 123 Ind.App. 609, 112 N.E.2d 872 (1953)   67 fn 13
Hamilton v State, 103 Ind. 96, 2 N.E. 299, 53 Am.Rep. 491 (1885)   49 fn 52
Owen d/b/a Clark's Greenhouse and Clark's Greenhouse, Inc. v The Kroeger Company, 936 F.Supp. 579 (S.D.Ind. 1996), 31 UCC Rep.Serv.2d 56   51 fn 60
Shank v Butsch, 28 Ind. 19, 1867 WL 2925 (Ind.)   21 fn 16
Zann v Haller, 71 Ind. 136, 1880 WL 6236 (Ind.), 23 Am.Rep. 193   27 fn 50

Iowa
Burns v Burrows, 196 N.W. 62, 196 Iowa 1048 (1923)   31 fn 83
Cummings v Landes, 117 N.W. 22, 140 Iowa 80 (1908)   49 fn 54
Loughren v B. F. Bonniwell & Co., 125 Iowa 518, 101 N.W. 287, 106 Am.St.Rep. 319 (1904)   61 fn 104

Kansas
Southwest Engineering Company, Inc. v Martin Tractor Company, Inc., 205 Kan. 684, 473 P.2d 18 (1970)   50–51 fn 59

Kentucky
Blackburn v City of Paducah, Ky., 441 S.W.2d 395 (1969)   73 fn 40
Blair v Campbell, 45 S.W. 93, 19 Ky.L.Rptr. 2012 (1898)   21 fn 17
Lamaster v Wilkerson, 143 Ky. 226, 136 S.W. 217 (1911)   51 fn 61

Table of cases   xix

Selma Savings Bank v Webster County Bank, 206 S.W. 870, 182 Ky.
604, 2 A.L.R. 1136 (1918)   73 fn 39
Stephens v Perkins, 273 S.W. 545 (1925)   21 fn 17
Wells v Lewis, 190 Ky. 626, 228 S.W. 3 (1921)   27 fn 53, 35 fn 113
Word v Whipps, 28 S.W. 151, 16 Ky. Law Rep. 403 (1894)   35–36 fn 113
Wurts v Newsome, 253 Ky. 38, 68 S.W.2d 448 (1934)   28 fn 59, 57 fn 86, 60 fn 98

Maine
Carlstrom, Re, 3 UCC Rep.Serv. 766, 1966 WL 8962 (Bank.D.Me.)   66 fn 7
Mahoney v Ayoob, 124 Me. 20, 125 A. 146, 37 A.L.R. 85 (1924)   61 fn 103
Maine League Federal Credit Union v Atlantic Motors, 250 A.2d 497,
6 UUC Rep.Serv. 198 (1969)   65 fn 4
Sawtelle v Wardwell, 56 Me. 146, 1868 WL 1770 (Me.)   27 fn 52

Maryland
Cambridge, Inc. v The Goodyear Tire & Rubber Company, 471 F.Supp.
1309 (1979)   65–66 fn 6
Drury v Young, 58 Md. 546, 1882 WL 4502 (Md.), 42 Am.Rep. 343   51 fn 60
Dubrowin v Schremp, 248 Md. 166, 235 A.2d 722 (1967)   66 fn 10

Massachusetts
Andre v Ellison, 324 Mass. 665 (1949), 88 N.E.2d 340   65 fn 4
Assessors of Boston v Neal, 311 Mass. 192, 40 N.E.2d 893 (1942)   67 fn 16
Boardman v Spooner, 13 Allen 353, 95 Mass. 353, 1866
WL 5009 (Mass.), 90 Am.Dec. 196   61 fn 102
Commonwealth v Ray, 3 Gray 441, 69 Mass. 441, 1855 WL 5701 (Mass.)   50 fn 56
Fessenden v Mussey, 65 Mass. 127, 1853 WL 4969 (Mass.)   26 fn 49
Foye v Patch, 132 Mass. 105, 1882 WL 10891 (Mass.)   22 fn 22
Hamdi Halal Mkt. LLC v United States, 947 F. Supp. 2d 159 (D. Mass. 2013)   66 fn 7
Henshaw v Foster, 9 Pick. 318, 26 Mass. 312, 1830 WL 25334 (Mass.)   51 fn 61
Irving v Goodimate, Co., 320 Mass. 454, 70 N.E.2d 414,
171 A.L.R. 326 (1946)   31 fn 83, 66 fn 10
Meads v Earle, 205 Mass. 553, 91 N.E. 916, 29 L.R.A.N.S. 63 (1910)   89 fn 4
Providence Granite Co., Inc. v Joseph Rugo, Inc., Mass. 291 N.E.2d 159,
362 Mass. 888 (1972)   73 fn 41
Sanborn v Flagler, 9 Allen 474, 91 Mass. 474, 1864 WL 3510 (Mass.)   31 fn 83
Walker v Walker, 175 Mass. 349, 56 N.E. 601 (1900)   26 fn 49
Wellington v Jackson, 121 Mass. 157, 1876 WL 10902 (Mass.)   50 fn 56
Wheeler v Lynde, 1 Allen 402, 83 Mass. 402, 1861 WL 6171 (Mass.)   61 fn 104

Michigan
Archbold v Industrial Land Co., 264 Mich. 289, 249 N.W. 858 (1933)   31 fn 83
Benedict Manufacturing Co. v Aeroquip Corp., 2004 WL 1532280,
53 UCC Rep.Serv.2d 888   51 fn 60
Borkowski v Kolodziejski, 332 Mich. 589, 52 N.W.2d 348 (1952)   31 fn 83
Etts v Deutsche Bank National Trust Company, 126 F.Supp.3d 889
(E.D.Mich. 2015)   67 fn 11
Grieb v Cole, 60 Mich 397, 27 N.W. 579, 1 Am.St.Rep. 533 (1886)   50–51 fn 59

MFS & Company, LLC v Caterpillar, Inc., 2011 WL 4693897, 75
    UCC Rep.Serv.2d 743 — 51 fn 60
Radke v Brendon, 271 Minn. 35, 134 N.W.2d 887 (1965) — 66 fn 10
Ryan v United States, 136 U.S. 68, 10 S.Ct. 913, 34 L.Ed. 447 (1890) — 73 fn 41

Minnesota
Ames v Schurmeier, 9 Minn. 221, 1864 WL 1409 (Minn.), 9 Gil. 206 — 49 fn 54
Brayley v Kelly, 25 Minn. 160, 1878 WL 3577 (Minn.) — 50 fn 57
Herrick v Morrill, 37 Minn. 250, 33 N.W. 849, 5 Am.St.Rep. 841 (1887) — 49 fn 54

Mississippi
Dawkins and Company v L & L Planting Company, 602 So.2d 838
    (Miss. 1992) — 51 fn 60, 66 fn 10
Sheehan v Kearney, 82 Miss. 688, 21 So. 41, 35 L.R.A. 102 (1936) — 23 fn 28
Town Council of Lexington v Union National Bank, 75 Miss.
    1, 22 So. 291 (1897) — 52 fn 65

Missouri
Defur v Westinghouse Electric Corporation, 677 F.Supp.622
    (E.D.Mo. 1988) — 22 fn 21, 50 fn 59
First Security Bank of Brookfield v Fastwich, 612 S.W.2d 799
    (Mo.App. 1981) — 65 fn 4
Great Western Printing Co. v Belcher, 127 Mo.App. 133,
    104 S.W. 894 (1907) — 26 fn 49, 86 fn 11
Kamada, M.D. v RX Group Limited, 639 S.W.2d 146 (Mo.App. 1982) — 31 fn 83
Kleine v Kleine, 219 S.W. 610, 281 Mo. 317 (1920) — 87 fn 13
Leesley Bros. v A. Rebori Fruit Co., 162 Mo.App. 195, 144 S.W. 138 (1912) — 73 fn 42
McKee v Vernon County, 3 Dill. 210, 16 F.Cas. 188, No. 8851 (1874) — 52 fn 65

Montana
Hillstrom v Gosnay, Mont., 614 P.2d 466 (1980) — 73 fn 41

Nebraska
Berryman v Childs, 98 Neb. 450, 153 N.W. 486 (1915) — 49 fn 53
Griffith v Bonawitz, 73 Neb. 622, 103 N.W. 327 (1905) — 29 fn 64
Hansen v Hill, 340 N.W.2d 8 (Neb. 1983), 215 Neb. 573 — 73 fn 41

New Hampshire
Grafton Bank v Flanders, 4 N.H. 239, 1827 WL 744 (N.H.) — 26 fn 47
Howley v Whipple, 48 N.H. 487 (1869) — 72 fn 37
Willoughby v Moulton, 47 N.H. 205, 1866 WL 1982 (N.H.) — 21 fn 16

New Jersey
Crabtree v Elizabeth Arden Sales Corporation, 305 N.Y. 48, 110
    N.E.2d 551 (1953) — 31 fn 83
First Valley Leasing, Inc. v Goushy, 795 F.Supp. 693 (D.N.J. 1992) — 51 fn 60
J. D. Loizeaux Lumber Company v Davis, 124 A.2d 593,
    41 N.J.Super. 231 (1956) — 66 fn 9
Madden v Hegadorn, 565 A.2d 725 (N.J.Super.L. 1989), 236 N.J.Super.
    280, affirmed 571 A.2d 296 (N.J. 1989), 239 N.J.Super. 268 — 83 fn 86

Table of cases   xxi

Matthews v Deane, 201 N.J.Super. 583, 493 A.2d 632 (1984)	51 fn 61
Smith v Howell, 11 N.J.Eq. 349, 1857 WL 4462 (N.J.Ch.), 3 Stockt. 349	31 fn 83

New Mexico

Costilla Estates Development Co. v Mascarenas, 33 N.M. 356, 267 P. 74 (1928)	61 fn 104
Watson v Tom Growney Equipment, Inc., 721 P.2d 1302 (N.M. 1986)	66 fn 10

New York

American Multimedia, Inc., In the Matter of v Dalton Packaging, Inc., 143 Misc.2d 295, 540 N.Y.S.2d 410 (1989)	83 fn 85
B & R Textile Corp. v Domino Textiles, Inc., 77 A.D.2d 539, 430 N.Y.S.2d 89, 29 UCC Rep.Serv. 396 (1980)	51 fn 60
Barnard v Heydrick, 49 Barb. 62, 32 How. Pr. 97, 2 Abb.Pr.N.S. 47 (1866)	49 fn 54
Bazak International Corp. v Mast Industries, Inc., 140 Ad.2d 211, 528 N.Y.S.2d 62, 6 UCC Rep.Serv.2d 375, appeal granted by 72 N.Y.2D 808, 529 N.E.2d 425, 533 N.E.2d 57 (N.Y. 1988), Order reversed by 73 N.Y.2D 113, 535 N.E.2d 633, 538 N.Y.2d 503, 57 USLW 2520, 82 A.L.R.4th 689, 7 UCC Rep.Serv.2d 1380 (N.Y. 1989)	83–84 fn 88
Brooklyn City Railroad Company v City of New York, 139 Misc. 691, 248 N.Y.S. 196 (1930)	60–61 fn 101
Brown v The Butchers & Drovers' Bank, 6 Hill 443, 41Am.Dec. 755 (1844)	86 fn 10
Butler v Benson, 1 Barb. 533 (1847)	22 fn 23
Cohen v Arthur Walker & Co., Inc., 192 N.Y.S. 228 (1922)	50–51 fn 59
Cohen v Wolgel, 107 Misc. Rep. 505, 176 N.Y.S. 764 affirmed 191 A.D. 883, 180 NY.S. 933 (1919)	66 fn 10
David v Williamsburgh City Fire Insurance Company, 83 N.Y. 265, 38 Sickels 265, 1880 WL 12653 (N.Y.), 38 Am.Rep. 418	26 fn 46
Dunning & Smith v Roberts, 35 Barb. 463 (1862)	73 fn 41
Farmers' Loan and Trust Company v Dickson, 9 Abb.Pr. 61 (1859)	49 fn 54
Galvin, In the Matter of the Estate of 78 Misc.2d 22, 355 N.Y.2d 751 (1974)	22 fn 23
Goldowitz v Henry Kupfer & Co., 80 Misc.Rep. 487, 141 N.Y.S. 531 (1913)	50–51 fn 59
Jackson v Jackson, 39 N.Y. 153, 12 Tiffany 153, 1868 WL 6249 (N.Y.)	22 fn 23
Jackson v Van Dusen, 5 Johns 144 (1809)	22 fn 23
La Mar Hosiery Mills, Inc. v Credit and Commodity Corporation, 28 Misc.2d 764, 216 N.Y.S.2d 186 (1961)	74 fn 43
Landeker v Co-operative Bldg. Bank, 130 N.Y. Supp. 780 (1911)	65 fn 5
McCready's Estate, 369 N.Y.S.2d 325, 82 Misc.2d 531 (1975)	24 fn 36
Mackay v J. and L. Bloodgood, 9 Johns. 285 (1812)	27 fn 51
Merchants' Bank, The v Spicer, 6 Wend. 443 (1831)	31 fn 82
Merritt v Clason, 12 Johns. 102, 7 Am.Dec. 286, 12 N.Y.S.C. 1814–15 92 affirmed as The Executors of Clason v Bailey, 14 Johns. 484 (1817)	86–87 fn 11
Mesibov, Glinert & Levy, Inc. v Cohen Bros. Mfg. Co. Inc., 245 N.Y. 305, 157 N.E. 148 (1927)	50–51 fn 59
Miller v Pelletier, 4 Edw. Ch. 102 (1975)	34 fn 103
Miller v Wells Fargo Bank International Corp., 406 F.Supp. 452 (1975)	78 fn 59
Palmer v Stevens, 1 Denio 471 (1845)	31 fn 81
Pearlberg v Levisohn, 112 Misc. 95, 182 N.Y.S. 615 (1920)	50–51 fn 59
Probate of the Will of Severance, Re, 96 Misc. 384, 161 N.Y.S. 452 (1916)	44 fn 25

Reich v Helen Harper, Inc., 3 UCC Rep.Serv. 1048, 1966 WL 8838
(N.Y.City Civ.Ct.)   50–51 fn 59
Romaniw's Estate, Re, 163 Misc. 481, 296 N.Y.S. 925 (1937)   21 fn 20
Stegman's Estate, Re, 133 Misc. 745, 234 N.Y.S. 239 (1929)   20 fn 11
Tenement House Department of City of New York v Weil, 76 Misc.
Rep. 273, 134 N.Y.S. 1062 (1912)   60–61 fn 101
Trevor v Wood, 9 Tiffany 307, 36 N.Y. 307, 1867 WL 6445 (N.Y.),
3 Abb.Pr.N.S. 355, 93 Am.Dec. 511, 1 Transc.App. 248 (1867)   73 fn 41
United Display Fixture Co., Inc. v S. & W. Bauman, 183 N.Y.S. 4 (1920)   50–51 fn 59
Vielie v Osgood, 8 Barb. 130 (1849)   50–51 fn 59
WPP Group USA, Inc. v The Interpublic Group of Companies, Inc.,
644 N.Y.S.2d 205, 228 A.D.2d 296 (1996)   83–84 fn 88

North Carolina
Devereux v McMahon, 108 N.C. 134, 12 S.E. 902, 12 L.R.A. 205 (1891)   21 fn 17
State v Byrd, 93 N.C. 624, 1885 WL 1753 (N.C.)   21 fn 19
State of North Carolina v Watts, 289 N.C. 445, 222 S.E.2d 389 (1976)   50 fn 58, 58 fn 89
Yaggy v The B.V.D. Company, Inc., 70 N.C.App. 590, 173 S.E.2d 496,
72 Am.Jur.2d (1970)   74 fn 44

North Dakota
Andre v North Dakota State Highway Commissioner, 295
N.W.2d 128 (1980)   60–61 fn 101
Hagen v Gresby, 159 N.W. 3, 34 N.D. 349, 5 L.R.A. 1917B, 281 (1916)   67 fn 13
State of North Dakota v Obrigewitch, 356 N.W.2d 105 (N.D. 1984)   60–61 fn 101

Ohio
Alarm Device Manufacturing Company v Arnold Industries, Inc.,
65 Ohio App.2d 256, Ohio App., 417 N.E.2d 1284 (1979)   51 fn 60

Oklahoma
Boyer v State, 68 Okl.Cr. 220, 97 P. 779 (1939)   50 fn 56
Moss v Arnold, 63 Okl.Cr. 343, 75 P. 491 (1938)   60–61 fn 101
State of Oklahoma ex rel. Independent School District Number One of Tulsa
County v Williamson, 352 P.2d 394 (Okla. 1960), 1960 OK 126   60–61 fn 101
State ex rel. West v Breckinridge, 34 Okla. 649, 126 P. 806, 1912 OK 283   73 fn 40

Oregon
Toon v Wapinitia Irrigation Co., 117 Or. 374, 243 P. 554 (1926)   50 fn 57

Pennsylvania
Appeal of Knox, 131 P. 220, 18 A. 1021, 6 L.R.A. 353,
17 Am.St.Rep. 798 (1890)   23 fn 29, 35–36 fn 113, 87 fn
Assay v Hoover, 5 Pa. St. 21 (1846)   22 fn 23, 24 fn 30
Brehony v Brehony, 289 Pa. 267, 137 A. 260 (1927)   25 fn 37
Brennan's Estate, Re 91, A. 220, 244 Pa. 574 (1914)   27 fn 54
Carna t/d/b/a T.C. Trucking Company v Bessemer Cement
Company, 558 F.Supp. 706 (1983)   49 fn 51
Commonwealth Department of Transportation v Ballard, 17 Pa. Cmwlth.
310, 331 A.2d 578 (1975)   61–62 fn 104

Grabill v Barr, 5 Pa. 441, 5 Barr. 441, 1846 WL 5049 (Pa.), 47 Am.Dec. 418	22 fn 23, 24 fn 30
Greenough v Greenough, 11 Pa.St. 497, 1849 WL 5732 (Pa.)	22 fn 23
Hessenthaler v Farzin, 564 A.2d 990 (Pa.Super. 1989)	74 fn 45
Kimmel's Estate, In re, 278 P. 435, 123 A. 405, 31 A.L.R. 678 (1924)	35–36 fn 113
Long v Zook, 13 Pa. 400, 1850 WL 5764 (Pa.), 1 Harris 400	22 fn 23
Main v Ryder, 84 Pa. 217, 4 W.N.C. 173, 1877 WL 13243 (Pa.)	22 fn 23
Ore & Chemical Corporation, The v Howard Butcher Trading Corp., 455 F.Supp. 1150 (1978)	78 fn 59
Plate's Estate, re 148 Pa. 55, 23 A. 1038 (1892)	6 fn 23, 34 fn 109
Robb v The Pennsylvania Company for Insurance on Lives and Granting Annuities, 40 W.N.C. 129, 3 Pa.Super. 254, 1897 WL 3989 (Pa.Super. 1897) affirmed by 186 Pa. 456, 40 A. 969	60 fn 96
Tabas v Emergency Fleet Corporation, 9 F.2d 648 affirmed United States Shipping Board Emergency Fleet Corporation v Tabas 22 F.2d 398 (1926)	65–66 fn 6
Tomilio v Pisco, 123 Pa. Super. 423, 187 A. 86 (1936)	21 fn 18, 23 fn 28
Vernon v Kirk, 30 Pa.St. 222 (1858)	24 fn 30
Zenith Radio Corporation v Matsushita Electric Industrial Co., Ltd, 505 F.Supp. 1190 (1980)	43 fn 24

South Carolina

Draper v Pattina, 29 S.C.L. 292, 2 Speers 292, 1844 WL 2584 (S.C.App.L.)	86–87 fn 11
Smith v Greenville County, 188 S.C. 349, 199 S.E. 416 (1938)	60–61 fn 101
Zimmerman v Sale, 37 S.C.L. 76, 3 Rich. 76, 1846 WL 2269 (S.C.App.L.)	21 fn 16

Tennessee

Brown v McClanahan, 68 Tenn. 347, 1878 WL 4292 (Tenn.), 9 Baxt. 347, 2 Leg.Rep. 59	21 fn 16

Texas

Adams v Abbot, 151 Tex. 601 (1952), 254 S.W.2d 78	73 fn 41
Barber, In re, 982 S.W.2d 364 (Tex. 1998)	61–62 fn 104
Barnes v Horne, 233 S.W. 859 (1921)	35–36 fn 113
Benavides v State of Texas, 763 S.W.2d 587 (Tex.App. – Corpus Christi 1988)	67 fn 15
B. F. Bridges & Son v First Nat. Bank of Center, 47 Tex.Civ.App. 454, 105 S.W. 1018 (1907)	61–62 fn 104
Britton, Ex parte, 382 S.W.2d 264 (1964)	61–62 fn 104
Brooks v The State of Texas, 599 S.W.2d 312 (1979)	60 fn 99
Cox Engineering, Inc. v Funston Machine and Supply Company, 749 S.W.2d 508 (Tex.App. 1988), 6 UCC Rep.Serv.2d 1399	51 fn 60
Estes v State, 484 S.W.2d 711 (1972)	61–62 fn 104
Hideca Petroleum Corporation v Tampimex Oil International Ltd., 740 S.W.2d 838 (Tex.App. – Houston [1st Dist.] 1987)	78 fn 59
Huff v The State of Texas, 560 S.W.2d 652 (1978)	61–62 fn 104
Kemp v State of Texas, 861 S.W.2d 44 (Tex.App. – Houston 14th Dist. 1993)	61–62 fn 104
Mortgage Bond Corporation v Haney, 105 S.W.2d 488 (1937)	22 fn 23

Parsons v The State of Texas, 429 S.W.2d 476 (1968)   61–62 fn 104
Paulus v The State of Texas, 633 S.W.2d 827 (Tex.Crim.App. 1981)   61–62 fn 104
Phillips v Najar, 901 S.W.2d 561 (Tex.App.-El Paso 1995)   53 fn 69
Short v Short, 67 S.W.2d 425 (1934)   22 fn 23
Spencer, Ex parte, 171 Tex.Cr.R. 339, 349 S.W.2d 727 (1961)   61–62 fn 104
Stork v State, 114 Tex.Crim. 398, 23 S.W.2d 733 (1930)   62 fn 106
Zaruba v Schumaker, 178 S.W.2d 542 (1944)   67 fn 17

Utah
Salt Lake City v Hanson, 19 Utah 2d 32, 425 P.2d 773 (1967)   60–61 fn 101
State of Utah v Montague, 671 P.2d 187 (Utah 1983)   61–62 fn 104

Vermont
Clossen v Stearns, 4 Vt. 11, 1831 WL 2104 (Vt.), 23 Am.Dec. 245   86 fn 10
Pike Industries, Inc. v Middlebury Associates, 398 A.2d 280 affirmed on other grounds 436 A.2d 725 cert denied 455 U.S. 947 (1992)   73 fn 41

Virginia
Clarke v Dunnavant, 10 Leigh 13, 37 Va. 13 (1839)   22 fn 23
Pilcher v Pilcher, 117 Va. 356, 84 S.E. 667, L.R.A. 1915D 902 (1915)   31 fn 85

Washington
Degginger v Martin, 48 Wash. 1, 92 P. 674 (1907)   31 fn 83

Wisconsin
Dreutzer v Smith, 56 Wis. 292, 14 N.W. 465 (1882)   61–62 fn 104
Finley v Prescott, 47 L.R.A. 695, 104 Wis. 614, 80 N.W. 930 (1899)   21 fn 19
Garton Toy Co. v Buswell Lumber & Mfg. Co., 150 Wis. 341, 136 N.W. 147 (1912)   66 fn 10
Kocinski v The Home Insurance Company, 154 Wis.2d 56, 452 N.W.2d 360 (Wis. 1990)   60 fn 100
Mezchen v More, 54 Wis. 214, 11 N.W. 534 (1882)   49 fn 54
Mueller's Will, Re, 188 Wis. 183, 205 N.W. 814, 42 A.L.R. 951 (1925)   20 fn 11
North American Seed Co. v Cedarburg Supply Co., 247 Wis. 31, 18 N.W.2d 466, 159 A.L.R. 250 (1945)   31 fn 86
Potts v Cooley, 13 N.W.Rep. 682 (1882)   50 fn 58
Will of Susan Jenkins, 43 Wis. 610, 1878 WL 3217 (Wis.)   22 fn 23

Wyoming
Iverson's Estate, Re, 39 Wyo. 482, 273 P. 684, 64 A.L.R. 203 (1929)   23 fn 28

Table of statutes

England and Wales

Bills of Exchange Act 1882	3 fn 12
Companies Act 1862	
s91	72
Companies Act 1985	
s368	81
Ecclesiastical Dilapidations Act 1871	
s35	56
s60	56
Housing Repairs and Rents Act 1954	59
Human Fertilisation and Embryology Act 1990	
sch 3	30–31
Interpretation Act 1978	6
Joint Stock Companies Arrangement Act 1870	
s2	72
Law of Property Act 1925	
s40	70
Law of Property (Miscellaneous Provisions) Act 1989	
s2(3)	30
Limitation Act 1980	
s7	76
s29(5)	76
s30	76
s30(1)	76
Local Government Act 1972	
s234(2)	59
Municipal Corporation Act 1853	
s32	30
s142	26
Parliamentary Voters Registration Act 1843	
s17	54
Public Health Act 1875	
s266	48
Railway and Canal Traffic Act 1854	
s7	46 fn 37
Sale of Goods Act 1893	
s4	47
Solicitors Act 1932	
s65	56
s65(2)(i)	56
Solicitors Act 1974	
s69(2)	37

Stamp Act 1891
    s80   71 fn 32
Statute of Frauds 1677
    s4   47, 75
    s17   46
Statute of Merchants 1285   16
Water Resources Act 1991
    (c 57) sch 4   6 fn 24
Wills Act 1837

Scotland

Conveyancing (Scotland) Act 1874   30 fn 78
Registration of Burgh Voters (Scotland) Act 1856
    s4   63
    sch A   63
Requirements of Writing (Scotland) Act 1995
    s7(2)   33

New Zealand

Contracts Enforcement Act 1956
    s2   30, 67

South Africa

Companies Act 1973   3

United States of America

Oklahoma

Uniform Facsimile Signature of Public Officials Act 62 O.S.Supp.1959   60 fn 101

Statutory instruments

Companies Act 1985 (Electronic Communication) Order 2000, SI 2000/3373   81
Insolvency Rules 1986, SI 1986/1925
    r 8.2(3)   79

Other enactments

England and Wales

County Court Rules 1889
    order VI, r 10   52

Singapore

Law Society Conditions of Sale 1981
    condition 29(2)   79
    condition (3)   79

1
An introduction to the signature

This monograph provides an historical consideration of the case law from common law jurisdictions relating to manuscript signatures, telegrams, facsimile transmissions and telex up to 1990. Judges in common law systems expanded the meaning of a signature as technologies developed and people used these new technologies in ways that were not anticipated. By recognizing that clear legal principles are not difficult to apply to new technologies, it follows that understanding electronic signatures and the various forms an electronic signature takes is also straightforward. The intention is to put the concept of the signature into a broad legal context, to set out the purposes that can be attributed to a signature and to explain the functions a signature is capable of performing. The function a signature performs remains as valid in the electronic age as when the use of an impression of a seal was considered to be the best means of authentication before the advent of widespread literacy, although seals, as with all other forms of evidence, could be forged.[1]

It is acknowledged that many of the cases referred to in this monograph refer to statutes that may well have been amended or appealed. However, this does not detract from the problems that lawyers and judges faced when applying legal principles to new forms of technology. As most of these cases illustrate, judges applied the underlying legal principles to the facts of the case, leaving the technology to one side, because the technology does not affect the legal principles. That judges and lawyers have had to deal with new technologies is hardly unique.

A signature can have a variety of purposes. For instance, painters in Renaissance Venice painted a signature on a painting in various ways and for a range of purposes – to provide for the authenticity of the painting or to assert that it was painted by a particular painter. It may also have been added by a leader of a workshop (who invariably was a famous painter) to indicate how they chose to represent themselves in relation to the conduct of their business, the determination of their reputation, and how they and their patrons perceived the value of their works[2] – indeed the signature was also there to reflect the quality of the work and the skill of the master.[3] For instance, the development of signatures on paintings in Venice during this period reflected developments in conceptions of the wider role of painters in the commercial and cultural world in Renaissance Venice. The painter would inscribe their signature on a painting, and might also include the date and other information, such as the name

---
1   R. G. Johnston, D. D. Martinez and A. R. E. Garcia, 'Were ancient seals secure?' (2001) 75 Antiquity 299.
2   Louisa C. Matthew, 'The painter's presence: signatures in Venetian Renaissance pictures' (1998) 80(4) The Art Bulletin 616, 620; see also Debra Pincus, 'Signatures of the Lombardo Workshop' (2013) 34(67) Artibus et Historiae 161; Lamia Balafrej, *The Making of the Artist in Late Timurid Painting* (Edinburgh University Press 2019), ch 5 'Wondrous Signature'.
3   Matthew, 'The painter's presence', 627.

of a patron and the site in which the artwork was to hang.[4] Signatures did not remain stable. From the 1440s, artists changed from using Gothic script to Roman script, and the style of the signature – in the way it was physically painted onto the painting – was intended to reveal the status of the artist.[5]

Another example is that of poets. While the print industry was in its infancy, and without the modern concept of intellectual property rights, poets took steps to assert authorship and to authenticate it at a time when printers had no qualms about printing the work of others without attribution.[6]

In Norman Sicily, signatures were intended to proclaim falsehoods and to conceal truths. For instance, the *'alāma* of King Roger was intended to give the impression that he was a Muslim ruler, and the *'alāmāt* of the eunuchs enabled them to conceal their faith from their Christian masters.[7]

Authentication can be the process by which a person or legal entity stresses the validity or genuineness of a particular piece of information. For instance, Professor Bedos-Rezak demonstrates that authenticity was, at one time, asserted by way of the style of writing:

> Bernard of Clairvaux (d. 1153) sought to reassure his correspondents about the authenticity and representativeness of two letters to which he was unable to affix his seal. In one letter, he wrote: 'I do not have my seal handy, but the reader will recognize the style because I myself have dictated the letter.' The other letter states: 'May the discursive structure stand for the seal, which I do not have handy.' Bernard expects readers to notice his personal presence, however immaterial, within the fabric of the text, through its style and diction.[8]

Alternatively, it can mean the formal assertion of validity, such as the signing of a certificate: we authenticate what it certifies. In certain circumstances, there may also be a need to verify the identity of an individual or legal entity, although what is meant by 'identity' will also depend on the reason for ascertaining the identity.[9] With a cheque, the signature serves to link the name of the person printed on the cheque with the person who claims to have the authority to draw money from the account indicated on the cheque.[10] In the past, the existence of the cheque guarantee card with a manuscript signature on the reverse served to reinforce the link between the card and the cheque, although the signature did not necessarily identify the person signing

---

4 Matthew, 'The painter's presence', 619.
5 Matthew, 'The painter's presence', 621–622.
6 For consideration regarding the evolution of being accredited as the author of poetry in the late medieval period in France, for instance, see Cynthia J. Brown, *Poets, Patrons, and Printers: Crisis of Authority in Late Medieval France* (Cornell University Press 1995), ch 4 'Changing Authorial Signatures in Late Medieval Works'.
7 Jeremy Johns and Nadia Jamil, 'Signs of the times: Arabic signatures as a measure of acculturation in Norman Sicily' (2004) 21 Muqarnas 181, 190.
8 Brigitte Miriam Bedos-Rezak, 'Medieval identity: a sign and a concept' (2000) 105(5) The American Historical Review 1489.
9 Nicholas Bohm and Stephen Mason, 'Identity and its verification' (2001) 26 Computer Law and Security Review 43; for a technical response, see R. E. Smith, *Authentication: from Password to Public Keys* (Addison-Wesley 2002).
10 Where the signature on a cheque appeared to be unqualified, see F. R. Malan, 'Composite signatures, personal liability and rectification' (1985) 3 J S Afr L 347; F. H. I. Cassim, 'The perplexing problem of company signatures on cheques – too little, too late' (2000) 117(4) S African L J 676.

the cheque, even if the signature on the reverse of the cheque guarantee card matched the signature on the cheque.[11] In cheque cases, the printed name on a cheque is not necessarily accepted as a form of signature, although it can contribute to authenticity. For instance, Lawton LJ considered the issue of authenticity in relation to a cheque with a name printed on it, and suggested that 'A printed name accompanied by a written signature was prima facie evidence that the cheque was being drawn on the account it purported to be drawn on',[12] although in the South African case of *Akasia Finance v Da Souza*[13] Leveson J indicated why, at 338 G–H, he did not consider the name printed on the cheque could be a signature:

> At the foot of each cheque, where the signature of the drawer is normally to be found, appear the words, 'Domestic Homes (Pty) Ltd, Registration No 73/0541'. The words are printed and are plainly printed by machine.
>
> It is well known that for several years past banks have been issuing cheque books to their customers with the customer's name machine-printed thereon in the same space as the cheques in the present case. The printing is usually computer-controlled. This is done as part of a design to facilitate the modern banking system. Of importance is the fact that the printing is not done by the customer. It is therefore not the company's signature in the sense that, if put there by a person authorised by a corporate customer, it would constitute the company's signature or seal under the provisions of the Companies Act 61 of 1973.

The function of a signature is generally determined by the nature and content of the document to which it is affixed.

It is thought that the act of a person fixing their name to a document is well understood by lawyers and non-lawyers alike. However, a consideration of the case law demonstrates the range of issues that have arisen in relation to what seems, at first glance, a relatively simple concept. The means by which judges have tested the validity of a signature has altered over time. From concentrating on the form a signature takes, judges went on to question its validity by considering the function the signature performs.[14] The analysis of the move from form to function applies equally to the analysis of electronic signatures. The perceptive comments from the sound dissenting judgment of Bell J in 1855 in the South African case of *Van Vuuren v Van Vuuren*,[15] at 121, provide a useful summary with which to begin:

> the expression 'to sign' a document has no strict legal or technical meaning different from the popular meaning, viz., to authenticate by that which stands for or is intended to represent the name of the person who is to authenticate. If

---

11 A website, sadly no longer available, (http://www.zug.com/pranks/credit_card/) illustrated how little people relied on a manuscript signature for the many millions of transactions conducted every day. The illustrations included the use of variations of their signature with a number of transactions, including evidence of the transaction slips.
12 *Ringham v Hackett* [1980] 1 WLUK 323, (1980) 124 SJ 201, Times, 9 February 1980, [1980] CLY 158, cited from (1980) 124 SJ 201 at 202(a). In *Central Motors (Birmingham) v PA & SNP Wadsworth (trading as Pensagain)* [1982] 5 WLUK 265, [1983] CLY 6u, [1982] CAT 231, 28 May 1982, (1983) 133 NLJ 555, a second account holder was held jointly liable for a cheque that he did not sign under the provisions of the Bills of Exchange Act 1882.
13 1993 (2) SA 337 (W).
14 Chris Reed, 'What is a signature?', (2000) 3 Journal of Information, Law and Technology (JILT), https://warwick.ac.uk/fac/soc/law/elj/jilt/2000_3/reed.
15 (1855) 2 Searle 116.

you say to the most illiterate person 'Sign this paper,' if he cannot write, he will put a cross to it, and if he do not know how to do this the most experienced man of business cannot tell him to do more. If the party have learned a little writing, or if rheumatism of hard labour have cramped the nerves of his hand, and you ask him to sign a document, he will put the initial capital letters of his Christian and surname, while he will not venture upon writing the other more minute and therefore more difficult to be executed letters of these names, and he will feel satisfied that he has 'signed'. If the man of business doubt this, and, seeing he can write so far as to be able to make the capital letters, think it will not be sufficient without the smaller letters, and insist upon his making them, should the party say he cannot, the lawyer will be content. On the other hand, should the party make the attempt and produce a scrawl more or less legible, so again the man of business will be content – whether the scrawl be legible or illegible, he will be satisfied that the man has 'signed'. Such is the popular and professional practice, and the decision of the Courts had been conformably to it.

Dictionary definitions

The *Oxford English Dictionary* offers a number of definitions of the word 'signature' as a noun and a verb.[16] The earliest references relate to signatures of a public nature that were intended to have legal effect. The first definition of a signature as a noun is that of 'A writing prepared and presented to the Baron of Exchequer by a writer to the signet, as the ground of a royal grant to the person in whose name it is presented'. An illustration for 1534 refers to 'To pass with writings and signaturis to be subscrivit be the Kingis grace'. The remaining references for this entry also relate to royal signatures in the public domain. The second and third definitions continue with the same meaning. Item 2(a) is defined as 'The name (or special mark) of a person written with his or her own hand as an authentication of some document or writing', and is illustrated from Hollyband of 1580, referring to 'the signature or marke of a Notaries', with the next illustration from Coke dated 1633 referring to 'A bill superscribed with the signature or signe manuall, or royall hand of the King'. The third reference, item 2(b), 'The action of signing one's name, or of authenticating a document by doing so', is also illustrated by an early reference to Lord Keeper Williams from 1621: 'Some things wee must offer to the kings signature when the clarkes are not to bee found.' The law dictionaries vary in their treatment of the definition of 'signature'.[17]

The manuscript signature

The epitome of a signature is the act of an individual writing their name in their own hand on a document, usually in the form of a manuscript signature.[18] More widely, it

---

16 *Oxford English Dictionary* (2nd edn on CD-ROM, version 4.0, 2009).
17 Bryan A. Gardner (ed.), *Black's Law Dictionary* (11th edn, West Group 2019); Daniel Greenberg (ed.), *Stroud's Judicial Dictionary of Words and Phrases* (11th edn, Sweet & Maxwell 2019); David Hay, *Words and Phrases Legally Defined* (5th edn, LexisNexis Butterworths 2018).
18 Although the *tuğra* (a cipher or imperial monogram) of the Ottoman sultans that served as the signature of the sultan was drawn up by a court official and affixed to official documents, over time it was also carved on seals and stamped on coins, and artists illuminated later *tuğra*. For a discussion of a *tuğra* of Suleiman the Magnificent, see Neil MacGregor, *A History of the World in 100 Objects* (Allen

is the action of a person affixing a permanent imprint upon a document. In the world before the invention of electricity and computers, an imprint was required to have the characteristic of permanency because it was necessary to retain tangible evidence of intention.[19] In addition, the parties to the document may consider it necessary to retain the evidence for a sufficient length of time in order to enforce any rights or obligations evidenced in the record.

Before the development of the telegraph, a document would normally be considered something written onto a material, mainly paper. Although a number of people may be involved with the framing of a document and its subsequent manifestation in its final physical form, the document will have been created physically. Thus if an instruction was passed from one party to another by means of the operators of a semaphore, the sending operator could give evidence of the instructions received from the instructing party and the signals they used to transmit the message, and the receiving operator could give evidence of the signals they observed and noted down on paper. With the development of communications over the electric telegraph, the same principles would apply as with the semaphore, but the electronic pulses would be interpreted in the light of the code used by the sending and receiving operators. The use of the telegraph meant that the message was encoded into electronic pulses, but these pulses were not stored. The receiving operator transferred the evidence of the message to a carrier (paper). In contrast, software code transmits and stores the data in digital form, but the data are not visible to the human eye. A combination of the interpretation and use of hardware and software are required to make the data visible to the human.

In a world that relied on physical and permanent evidence of proof of intent, the requirement for an enduring record is understandable. While the legal consequences of a signature will differ when fixed to artefacts, such as items of pottery, paintings, sculpture and carvings on surfaces such as stone,[20] marble, glass and wooden furniture, nevertheless a signature is capable of establishing the identity of the creator of the article and is also capable of authenticating the provenance of the object.[21]

Lane 2010), 71 'Tughra of Suleiman the Magnificent', 458–463; for illustrations of *tuğra*, see M. Uğur Derman, *Masterpieces of Ottoman Calligraphy from the Sakip Sabanci Museum* (Sabanci University, Sakip Sabanci Museum, 2004).
19 Note the research presently being conducted by the School of History and Heritage at the University of Lincoln entitled: 'Imprint. A Forensic and Historical Investigation of Fingerprints on Medieval Seals'. This research is a collaboration between history and forensic science, using a range of methods for hand mark identification, including digital imaging and the analysis of marks using both manual and Automated Fingerprint Identification System techniques of between 1,200 and 1,500 medieval seals which are still associated with their parent documents. Already, fingerprints and palm prints have been identified as a result of the process of affixing the seal: https://gtr.ukri.org/projects?ref=AH%2FM010813%2F1.
20 For a discussion relating to the most beautiful mausoleum that exists on earth, see Ebba Koch, *The Complete Taj Mahal and the Riverfront Gardens of Agra* (Thames & Hudson 2006), 90–91; Syed Ali Nadeem Rezavi, 'Builders of the Taj: Evidence of the Stone-Cutter's Marks' (2012) 73 Proceedings of the Indian History Congress 408.
21 The copy of a painting with a false signature painted on it with the intention of passing off the painting as having been created by the named painter was determined to be a cheat at common law by the Cockburn LCJ and his fellow judges in *Regina v Thomas Closs* (1858) Crown Cases Reserved 460, Dears & Bell 460.

A document usually exists on a carrier, typically paper. The carrier is marked permanently with content, usually with ink, either in the form of handwriting or by mechanical means, such as a printing press, typewriter or printer. This process alters the carrier physically. The content imprinted on the carrier may include a range of information, depending on the nature of the document, including information about the person that created, issued or initiated the content. Over time, as it is handled, the carrier will include additional information, including water, coffee or tea stains, scratches, additional content, fingerprints and DNA. Finally, a person or legal entity might sign the carrier with a signature. The reason for signing the document will depend on the nature of the document and the purpose for which the person is signing. When brought together, these components comprise the document in its entirety.[22]

Statutory definition of signature

There does not appear to be a statutory definition of the term 'signature', and Ashman J commented in 1892 in a case regarding probate that there was no judicial formula either:

> Exactly what constitutes a signature has never been reduced to a judicial formula ... The principle upon which these cases proceeded was that whatever the testator of grantor was shown to have intended as his signature was a valid signing, no matter how imperfect or unfinished or fantastical or illegible, or even false, the separate characters or symbols he used might be, when critically judged.[23]

The Interpretation Act 1978 does not provide a definition, although Professor Reed noted there were fifteen statutory definitions of 'signature' or 'signing' in force in 1996, eleven of which adopted an identical or similar variation to the following: ' "signature" includes a facsimile of a signature by whatever process reproduced'.[24] This particular definition is sufficiently general to include a representation of a signature in electronic form. The most obvious example is that of a manuscript signature that is scanned and converted into digital form. Such a representation can be attached to a document produced on a computer, or it could be the image of the signature as sent and received by a facsimile machine. It is estimated that there are in the region of 40,000 references to the requirement for a manuscript signature in English legislation.[25] However, whether a personal signature is required depends upon the wording of the statute or the context of the requirement.[26] With respect to legislation, Professor Reed notes that the statutory provisions relating to signatures fall into three broad categories:

> Where documents that have been signed are admissible in evidence, or create evidential presumptions. The evidential presumptions are either that the

---

22 For the meaning of a 'document', see Stephen Mason, 'Documents signed or executed with electronic signatures in English law' (2018) 34(4) Computer Law and Security Report 933.
23 Mitchell J quoted these comments of Ashman J (whose decision was reversed) in *In re Plate's Estate*, 148 Pa. 55, 23 A. 1038 (1892).
24 Water Resources Act 1991 (c 57) Schedule 4, Part II, Proceedings of Flood Defence Committees, quoted in Chris Reed, *Digital Information Law: Electronic Documents and Requirements of Form* (Centre for Commercial Studies, 1996), 225; Table 5.1, 262-263 for the full list.
25 HC Official Report (6th series) col 41, 29 November 1999; note also Reed, *Digital Information Law*, 239 and n. 41; Reed, 'What is a signature?', 3.1.2 and n. 68.
26 Reed, *Digital Information Law*, 233-244 and nn. 23 and 24.

document is conclusive proof of its contents, or it is clear evidence of the facts set out in the document.

Where documents have to be signed for the purpose of authentication, either expressly or from the context of the requirement.

Where a signature is required to exercise a statutory power.[27]

Humans have relied on the signature, or a form of signature, for thousands of years. This naturally leads into a discussion of the functions a signature is capable of performing, which are covered in the next chapter.

---

27 Reed, *Digital Information Law*, 240–241. Professor Reed provides examples at 42–52.

2
The functions of a signature

In the legal context, a signature can serve a number of functions, each of which can have varying degrees of importance,[1] including complying with a legal requirement that something be signed.

The primary evidential function

It is suggested that the primary purpose of a signature serves to provide admissible and reliable evidence that comprises the following elements:

> (1) To provide tangible evidence that the signatory approves and adopts the contents of the document.
>
> (2) In so doing, the signatory agrees that the content of the document is binding upon them and will have legal effect.
>
> (3) Further, the signatory is reminded of the significance of the act and the need to act within the provisions of the document.

The nature of the act of signing differs between the application of a manuscript signature and the use of an electronic signature. This is because a manuscript signature, if authentic, is biologically linked to a specific individual, but cryptographic authentication systems bind signatures to individuals by way of software code and procedural mechanisms.

---

1   Lon L. Fuller, 'Consideration and form' (1941) 41 Columbia Law Review 799 refers to the evidentiary, cautionary and channelling functions; Ashbel G. Gulliver and Catherine J. Tilson, 'Classification of gratuitous transfers' (1941) 51 Yale Law Journal 1; John H. Langbein, 'Substantial compliance with the Wills Act' (1975) 88(3) Harvard Law Review 489; Mark Sneddon, 'Legislating to facilitate electronic signatures and records: exceptions, standards and the impact on the statute book' (1998) 21 University of New South Wales Law Journal, part 2 II A (i)–(iv), http://www.austlii.edu.au/au/journals/UNSWLJ/1998/59.html; 'Digital signature guidelines' (Judicial Studies Board 2000), 3; Jos Dumortier, Patrick Van Eecke and Ilse Anné, *The Legal Aspects of Digital Signatures* (Leuven: Interdisciplinary Centre for Law and Information Technology 1998), Report 1, Part III, 50; ISTEV, 'Legal and regulatory Issues for the European trusted services infrastructure – European trusted services' (2007), para 3; *Digital Signature Guidelines* (American Bar Association 1996), 49; Adrian McCullagh, Peter Little and William Caelli, 'Electronic signatures: understand the past to develop the future' (1998) 21 University of New South Wales Law Journal 56; UNCITRAL Model Law on Electronic Commerce with Guide to Enactment 1996 with additional article 5 bis as adopted in 1998 (New York: United Nations, 1999) paras 48 and 53; UNCITRAL Model Law on Electronic Signatures with Guide to Enactment 2001 (United Nations, New York 2002) para 29; 'Protections of the acknowledgment' in 'A Position on Digital Signature Laws and Notarization', a position statement from the National Notary Association, September 2000, 3–5; *Promoting Confidence in Electronic Commerce: Legal Issues on International Use of Electronic Authentication and Signature Methods* (Vienna: United Nations, 2009), 1–8; for a similar overview of the same topic and discussion of the development of signatures, see Lorna Brazell, *Electronic Signatures and Identities Law and Regulation* (3rd edn, Sweet & Maxwell 2018), 2001–2006.

With electronic signatures, the person does not physically sign anything, but causes software to sign electronically using a machine that cannot be relied on to know what document has been signed[2] – even when using a biodynamic version of a manuscript signature. This is significant, because the act of signing using an electronic signature has a different symbolic meaning to that of a manuscript signature, and suggests a weaker sense of the involvement of the person in the process of signing, as noted by Professor Chou.[3]

Secondary evidential functions

A signature can also provide evidence of identification and proof of the following:

> (1) Authentication of the identity of the person signing the document. One example would be to reinforce the causal link between the signature and a name printed on a document, such as a name printed on a cheque book or credit card.
>
> (2) The identity of a particular characteristic, or attribute or status of the person, such as a government minister or company director.
>
> (3) That a person signing acknowledges, verifies or witnesses the content of the document, but does not necessarily agree to be bound by it.
>
> (4) That existence of the document provides a record of the intent of the signatory and, in turn, physical evidence of the originality and completeness of the document itself, including the time, date and place of the act of the affixing of the signature to the document.
>
> (5) The authenticity and voluntary nature of the signature of a third party where a person is a witness to the signing of a document, and affixes their own signature as confirmation of this.
>
> (6) Demonstration that the content of the document has not been altered subsequently to the affixing of the signature.
>
> (7) Evidence that the record is a true copy of another record.
>
> (8) Confirmation of the receipt of something, or to obtain access to something.

Cautionary function

This function acts to reinforce the legal nature of the document, thereby warning the person affixing their signature that they should take care before committing themselves to the contents of the document.

Protective function

As a corollary to the cautionary function, the party receiving the document containing a manuscript signature recognizes that the other party affirms the content of the

---

2   Stephen Mason and Timothy S. Reiniger, '"Trust" between machines? Establishing identity between humans and software code, or whether you know it is a dog, and if so, which dog?' (2015) 21 Computer and Telecommunications Law Review 135.
3   E. Y. Chou, 'Paperless and soulless: e-signatures diminish the signer's presence and decrease acceptance' (2015) 6 Social Psychological and Personality Science 343. Professor Chou also provides further citations.

document and they have given their full attention to that content. They can also be assured of the identity of the signatory, and are consequently in receipt of proof of the source and contents of the document. This function is linked to the evidential function.[4]

Channelling function

The formality of a manuscript signature helps to clarify the point at which a person recognizes the act has become legally significant. Also, the content of the document, by being recorded on a durable form, serves to concentrate the mind on the legally binding nature of the document, thus reducing the risks associated with oral recollections. This function is also linked to the evidential function.

Record-keeping function

Closely related to the evidential function, a document contained on a carrier manifest in physical form serves as a durable record of the terms of the agreement. It also enables governments to impose taxes on documents and permits audits based on documents that have a physical existence.

---

4   Sneddon, 'Legislating to facilitate electronic signatures and records', Part 2 II A (ii).

3
Disputing a manuscript signature

Defences

A manuscript signature cannot be disputed unless the following defences can be established: the signature is a forgery;[1] the signature was conditional; the signature was obtained as a result of misrepresentation; the signature was obtained in such circumstance that it was not the act of the person signing (*non est factum*); mental incapacity; mistake; where one party unilaterally added material terms to the writing after the other's signature; where the person signing the document did not realize the document they signed was a contractual document; by statute as being unreasonable or unfair. These defences are not dealt with here, other than a brief consideration of the disputes where a manuscript signature has been at issue. The reader is referred to the standard textbooks on the subject.

It is well known that manuscript signatures are often forged. To prevent this problem, and to test both the validity and the effectiveness of a manuscript signature, some documents require the signature to be affixed in the presence of a witness or an authorized official, such as a notary.

Evidence of the manuscript signature

Should a manuscript signature recorded in a document be challenged, evidence will need to demonstrate the issues discussed below. It should be noted that the evidential burden is a factor in considering the precise nature of the signature. In the Canadian case of *Regina v Blumes*,[2] the signature on a vehicle registration document issued by the Insurance Corporation of British Columbia was challenged. It was alleged that the document was not admissible because it was not clear whether the signature was a manuscript signature, a rubber stamp or a facsimile signature. This document was afforded the presumption of regularity, which meant that a mere challenge was not sufficient to avoid the operation of regularity.

---

1 In the case of *Brown v National Westminster Bank Ltd* [1964] 2 Lloyd's Rep 187, [1964] 6 WLUK 133, [1964] CLY 191, the bank paid sums of money on 329 cheques that were alleged to contain forged copies of Mrs Brown's signature. The bank admitted to paying out on 100 cheques that were forged, but put Mrs Brown to proof that the remaining cheques were forged. This was because the bank took measures, through the branch managers, to question Mrs Brown on a number of cheques that passed through her account. Mrs Brown failed to prove that she did not sign the remaining cheques. For similar facts in Australia, see *Tina Motors Pty. Ltd. v Australia and New Zealand Banking Group Ltd.* [1977] VR 205.
2 2002 BCPC 45.

The identity of the person affixing the manuscript signature

Evidence will have to be adduced to show the signature affixed to the document is that of the signatory. In such cases, the signature in question will have to be compared to samples of the same signature. A signature may be forged, or the signature could be that of the signatory but they may have attempted to disguise their handwriting. Thus a handwriting analyst[3] will need to have two kinds of samples: 'request samples' which are produced for the examination and duplicate the material in question, and naturally occurring samples made by the signatory without realizing the example will be examined. Two main factors can then be examined: that of pictorial impression, which includes matters such as slope, size, margins, spacing and the position of the writing in relation to lines, and then the way in which letters are constructed, such as the direction in which the letter 'o' is formed, the way the letter 't' is crossed and the way in which the person has written letters that require more than one movement. Forgers tend to concentrate on the pictorial impression and fail to copy details of the way letters are constructed. Likewise, people trying to disguise their handwriting also concentrate on the pictorial impression, rather than changing the formation of their letters. Further analysis can be undertaken by considering the relative proportions of letters, the spaces between letters and pressure variations. The attributes of the instrument used to affix the signature to the document can also be considered, such as how smoothly the signature has been written, whether it is jagged or confident, whether there is a pause and where the instrument lifts off the surface.

The carrier itself can be examined, from the type of material used (physical properties, optical properties), any security features (watermarks), the printing process used (the use and identification of a photocopier, computer or printer) and other evidence such as perforations and microscopic analysis that might reveal imperfections that may link the carrier to the person. Further examination can include the comparison of typescript; impressions by means of Electrostatic Detection Apparatus; whether more than one type of material was used to affix information on the carrier; whether any alterations were made or entries obliterated, and the sequence in which intersecting lines have been written.[4]

Where the party relying on the authenticity of the manuscript signature successfully demonstrates the similarity of the manuscript signature to the sample signatures, the evidential burden will then fall upon the alleged signatory to prove the signature was forged. The principle also applies to a forged signature, as noted in *Saunders v Anglia Building Society (formerly Northampton Town and County Building Society)*.[5] In this

---

3   Recent research has demonstrated that the findings of experts across all forensic disciplines can be subject to bias as the result of cognitive factors, such that the same expert has reached the opposite conclusion with the same evidence, for which see Itiel D. Dror, Christophe Champod, Glenn Langenburg, David Charlton, Heloise Hunt and Robert Rosenthal, 'Cognitive issues of fingerprint analysis: inter- and intra-expert consistency and the effect of a "target" comparison' (2011) 208 Forensic Science International 10 and the references cited therein. Apparently the US Secret Service uses a software program called Forensic Information System for Handwriting (FISH) that enables document examiners to scan and digitize text writings such as threatening correspondence.
4   Jennifer L. Mnookin, 'Scripting expertise: the history of handwriting identification evidence and the judicial construction of reality' (2001) 87(8) Virginia Law Review 1723.
5   [1971] AC 1004, [1970] 3 WLR 1078, [1970] 3 ALL ER 961, [1970] 11 WLUK 45, [1971] 22 P & CR 300, (1970) 114 SJ 885, Times, 10 November 1970, [1971] CLY 1805.

case the signature was obtained in such circumstance that it was not the act of the person signing.

Intention to authenticate and adopt the document

Where a person affixes their manuscript signature to a document, it must be shown that they intended to sign the document. The case of *L'Estrange v F Graucob Limited*,[6] which pre-dates the modern legislation, serves to illustrate the point. In this case, Miss L'Estrange carried on the business of a café. The defendants manufactured and sold automatic slot machines. In early 1933, Miss L'Estrange agreed to buy an automatic slot machine for cigarettes for a total of £81 5s 6d, payable over eighteen months. She signed a form, printed on brown paper and headed 'Sales Agreement'. This document included a number of contract terms written in very small print, one of which included the words 'This agreement contains all the terms and conditions under which I agree to purchase the machine specified above, and any express or implied condition, statement, or warranty, statutory or otherwise not stated herein is hereby excluded'. The machine was installed on 2 March 1933. However, it failed to work, and she eventually initiated an action in the county court to recover the payments she had made. Judgment was made in her favour. The decision was reversed in the Divisional Court because Miss L'Estrange had signed the written contract, and in doing so had acknowledged that she was bound by the terms. There was no misrepresentation that induced her to sign. It was irrelevant that she did not read the contract or know its contents.[7]

Representing the signature of another in a document, rather than signing with your own name, can be fraught with difficulties. In *Pryor v Pryor*,[8] Anthony Pryor made a will on 5 November 1859. One of the attesting witnesses was his daughter. The testator wanted his daughter's husband to sign the will as a witness, but because it was not known when he would return, he asked his daughter to sign her husband's name instead of her own. She did so. Sir C Creswell refused to admit the will to probate because the subscription was not intended to represent her signature.

Although a manuscript signature on a document may not be in dispute, the person signing the document may wish the other party to infer they had the authority to sign the document, as in the case of *Ringham v Hackett*.[9] This presumption may be rebutted by evidence. In *Ringham*, the name printed on the cheque was that of a partnership, and the signature by one of the partners on the cheque was deemed to be sufficient evidence to intend the recipient to infer the cheque was drawn on the partnership. In the case of *Central Motors (Birmingham) v PA & SNP Wadsworth (trading as Pensagain)*,[10] Central Motors required a cheque for the payment for a motor car in

---

6 [1934] 2 KB 394, [1934] 2 WLUK 22; J. R. Spencer, 'Signature, consent, and the rule in *L'Estrange v Graucob*' CLJ, 104, notes at 104 that this was not the first case in which the rule was laid down, although it was the case that made the rule famous; see *Parker v The South Eastern Railway Company* (1877) 2 CPD 416, *Luna, The Frances & Jane, The Luna, The* [1920] P 22, (1919) 1 Ll L Rep 475, [1919] 12 WLUK 19 also known as: *Frances & Jane, The v Luna, The*, and *Blay v Pollard and Morris* [1930] 1 KB 628.
7 This decision and the discussion of a fourth defence – that the signatory did not agree to the term – is set out in Spencer, 'Signature, consent, and the rule in *L'Estrange v Graucob*'.
8 (1860) LJR 29 NS P, M & A 114.
9 [1980] 1 WLUK 323, (1980) 124 SJ 201, Times, 9 February 1980, [1980] CLY 158.
10 [1982] 5 WLUK 265, [1983] CLY 6u, [1982] CAT 231, 28 May 1982, (1983) 133 NLJ 55.

the name of the firm Pensagain. In accordance with this request, Mr Wadsworth gave Central Motors a cheque with his signature beneath the name of the firm, which was printed on the cheque below that of the names of the defendants. It was held that by handing over a cheque signed in this way, Mr Wadsworth provided sufficient evidence from the circumstances to personally authenticate the document as being a cheque of the firm. By signing the cheque, Mr Wadsworth had the requisite intent to adopt the cheque as that of the firm.

4
Methods of authentication before manuscript signatures

Objects as a means of authentication

Before the use of written charters became common, objects would be used to preserve memory and provide evidence of an act, especially when obtaining title to a property. The object served as a symbol of the conveyance. For instance, Earl Warenne gave a gift to Lewes Priory in 1147, and both he and his brother had hair from their head cut off by Henry of Blois, bishop of Winchester before the altar for retention by the Priory as evidence of the gift,[1] although by the reign of Henry II judges began to refuse to take cognizance of symbolic objects other than sealed writings. However, the production of an object could still be adduced as evidence, and knives were used for this purpose, especially for a conveyance.[2]

The seal

In England, there was a time when a personal signature was not accepted as a lawful mark of authentication on a document unless the person signing the document was a Jew. A Christian was required to sign with a cross, or their signum was affixed to the document in the form of an impression of a seal.[3] Seal impressions were made in malleable metals, such as gold or silver, while the papacy used lead. The use of metals prevented the impression from being attached directly to the document, which meant the seal had to be attached to the document in some other way, such as with a piece of string. Sealing wax, which is an amalgam of beeswax and resin, then began to be used. Beeswax becomes malleable when gently heated, and resin acts as an adhesive. In the sixteenth century, shellac was introduced as a seal material, and remains popular today. By 1300 in England, the use of seals had permeated society to such an extent that serfs and villeins were using documents, especially to convey property. The use of seals has a long history in many parts of the world, including China, Japan and Korea, where they continue to be used daily.[4]

---

1 M. T. Clanchy, *From Memory to Written Record: England 1066–1307* (2nd edn, Blackwell 1993), 38, where further examples are given.
2 Clanchy, *From Memory to Written Record*, 39, 257–259 indicating knives were often used to convey land, and the blade had to be broken in the process.
3 Clanchy, *From Memory to Written Record*, 233; P. D. A. Harvey and A. McGuinness, *A Guide to British Medieval Seals* (University of Toronto Press 1996), 1. P. M. Barnes and L. C. Hector, *A Guide to Seals in the Public Record Office* (2nd edn, HMSO 1968) illustrates on page 3 that the meaning of 'seal' is the actual impression that was attached to a document, and the 'matrix' or 'die' is the implement which makes the impression. The words 'matrix' and 'die' will not be used for fear of making the subject far too technical.
4 For the importance of the Great Seal in the political context, see Hugh Hanley, '"The last shadow": negotiating the Great Seal and direct access to the king, 1931' (2015) 26 Irish Studies in International Affairs 257; Peter Walne, 'The Great Seal deputed of Virginia' (1958) The Virginia Magazine of History and Biography 3; Gwilyn Dodd, 'Trilingualism in the medieval English bureaucracy: the use – and

Witnesses and scribes

Clanchy has observed that there would be occasions when the addition of the sign of the cross or the impression of a seal on a charter was not considered a sufficient means of authentication. Hence documents would include a list of witnesses attending the event in which the promise was made. In such cases, the emphasis would have been on the public ceremonial attendant upon the transaction.[5] It was also possible that parties would rely on the particular handwriting of a scribe to establish the authenticity of a document.[6] The test of distinctive handwriting was acknowledged in the Statute of Merchants of 1285, requiring all merchants to have their debts recorded before the mayor of London, or before similar authorities in other cities and towns, as designated. Each bond was to be written by a nominated clerk, and the bond had to be enrolled in the hand of the clerk who was known to the persons to whom the bond was addressed. The handwriting of the clerk acted to authenticate the text written in the bond.[7]

Iris Agmon observed a similar practice in the Jaffa court records, where the act of authentication was solely for the purposes of the court:

> Prior to the 1879 regulations, a significant characteristic of the practice of signing records, mostly registrations, as inscribed in the Jaffa court records, is that it was often the scribe who signed on behalf of the person whose signature was needed. Hence, it seems that the court documents were rendered official by the format of the title of the signatory and the name written below this title by the scribe, and not by the authentic handwriting of this person. Sometimes the title alone without the person's name sufficed. This format, when attached to the relevant record written by a court scribe in a volume of court records, validated the document as an official record of the court. It is worth noting in this regard that the purpose of these signatures was not to approve the content of the record or its authenticity outside the court, for these records would be preserved only by the court personnel.[8]

---

disuse – of languages in the fifteenth-century Privy Seal Office' (2012) 51(2) Journal of British Studies 253; for discussion of where a seal was forged to falsely represent that a painting was by a particular painter, see Yu Leqi, 'A problem of attribution: a rediscovered Chinese landscape painting in the University of Pennsylvania Museum' (2017) 72 Arts Asiatiques 153; further items of interest include: Lamia Balafrej, *The Making of the Artist in Late Timurid Painting* (Edinburgh University Press 2019), ch 5 'Wondrous Signature'; Li Xueqin, (trs) K. C. Chang, *Eastern Zhou and Qin Civilizations* (Yale University Press 1985); Susan M. Johns, *Noblewomen, Aristocracy and Power in the Twelfth-Century Anglo-Norm Realm* (Manchester University Press 2003), ch 7 'Seals'; Brigitte Miriam Bedos-Rezak, *Seals – Making and Marking Connections across the Medieval World* (Arc Humanities Press 2018); W. P. Wallace, 'The Public Seal of Athens' (1949) 3(2) Phoenix 70; Lothar Wagner, 'Art as an instrument for political legitimation during the Tang: "The small seal script and the legitimation seal"' (1997) 40(2) Oriens Extremus 159.
5   Clanchy, *From Memory to Written Record*, 295.
6   On the forgery of early charters, see Christopher N. L. Brooke, 'Approaches to medieval forgery' (1968) 8(38) Journal of the Society of Archivists 377; Bruce O'Brien, 'Forgery and the literacy of the early common law' (1995) 27(1) Albion: A Quarterly Journal Concerned with British Studies 1; Alfred Hiatt, *The Making of Medieval Forgeries: False Documentation in Fifteenth-Century England* (The British Library 2004); David Cannadine (ed.), *Westminster Abbey: A Church in History* (Paul Mellon Centre for Studies in British Art in association with The Dean and Chapter of the Collegiate Church of St Peter Westminster 2019), 14–15, 16, 17, 21, 34–35, 46, 363–364, 381.
7   Clanchy, *From Memory to Written Record*, 307; see also F. W. Shipley, 'The Vatican Codex of Livy's third decade and its signatures' (1910) 4(4) The Classical Quarterly 277.
8   Iris Agmon, 'Recording procedures and legal culture in the late Ottoman Shari'a court of Jaffa, 1865–1890' (2004) 11(3) Islamic Law and Society 333, 353.

Such documents were copied into the court records word for word in their totality, and attempts were made to imitate the shape of the text on the original paper, including signatures and seals. It is suggested that this practice was linked to the centrality of the ambivalence of Islamic law regarding the reliability of written documents. Islamic legal doctrine regarded oral testimony generally as more reliable than written texts: 'Apparently, by imitating the shape of the original document, the scribe was attempting to render the written text in terms of its orality, as if the exact reconstruction of the original shape of the text was a trace of the oral testimony or instruction given by its author in court.'[9]

The sign of the cross

The presumption about what constitutes a signature is predicated on the concept of literacy. Evidence from anthropological studies of non-literate societies and sociological studies of people living in deprived areas of the industrialized world suggests that literacy itself is primarily a form of technology.[10] This is reflected in the history of literacy, because in medieval society it was rare for the most educated people to know how to write. There was no value placed on a personal signature. Documents were ratified with a cross, because the cross was a solemn symbol of Christian truth. This method of authentication was retained after the conquest of England by the Normans in 1066,[11] and is illustrated in a grant dated 1068–76 by Waleran of property at Bures St Mary, Suffolk, to St Stephen's Abbey, Caen, attested by William I, Queen Matilda, John of Bayeaux, bishop of Rouen, and Roger and Robert Beaumont, with their names added by the scribe next to each cross.[12]

The chirograph

Sometimes two copies of a document, whatever the subject, would be produced. This form of document was known as a chirograph, dating from the ninth century or earlier. A chirograph might record an agreement between two parties, including a marriage settlement, conveyance of land or repayment of a loan. The text was written twice, usually on the two halves of one side of a piece of parchment. When written on the same parchment, the two halves were separated by being torn or cut into two pieces, usually with the edges forming a wavy line or a zigzag as a precaution against forgery or alteration.[13] In addition, the scribe would add text across the division, such as the word

---

9   Agmon, 'Recording procedures and legal culture', 354–355.
10 Clanchy, *From Memory to Written Record*, 7.
11 W. S. Holdsworth, *A History of English Law*, III (3rd edn, Methuen), 231.
12 Harvey and McGuinness, *A Guide to British Medieval Seals*, figure 1. Museums across the world display early documents, and it is fun to seek out such documents to note the various designs of a cross that people adopted. Two documents from the state archive of Dubrovnik on display in the Dubrovnik maritime museum show a variety of crosses: a contract between Dubrovnik and Termoli from 1203, signed in Termoli on the mutual exemption from port duties and taxes; an agreement on the renewal of friendship between Dubrovnik and Molfetta from 1208, confirming mutual exemption from port duties and taxes as stated in the previous contract from 1148.
13 In a similar fashion, after being notched with the amount received, tally sticks were cracked open lengthways by splitting the stick vertically into two. The tally-writer then inscribed the smooth sides

CHIROGRAPHUM.[14] Each party would be given one of the halves of the parchment, duly authenticated by the impression of the seal of the other party, and each piece served to authenticate the other. This practice was so popular that chirographs became known as indentures. Tripartite chirographs were also widely used in England for drawing up wills in the tenth and eleventh centuries.[15]

with the details of the person to whom the tally was given and the reason for the payment. Samuel Pepys describes being nominated as Treasurer of the Committee of Tanger (now Tangiers), and indicates that he was 'put into a condition of striking of Tallys': 20 March 1665. As a record, they were light, small and virtually impossible to forge. To make space in the rambling buildings making up the Palace of Westminster, the Treasury ordered any tally sticks no longer being used as records to be destroyed. In burning the tally sticks in the furnaces that heated the House of Lords, the heat generated was so great as to cause the House of Lords and House of Commons to burn to the ground (Caroline Shenton, *The Day Parliament Burned Down* (Oxford University Press 2012), 14–15; 50–53, 240).
14   Clanchy, *From Memory to Written Record*, 87; for an example of an agreement between Colchester Abbey and the burgesses dating from 1254, see plate VII in the Harvard Law Library MS 87, 2.254.
15   Pierre Chaplais, *English Diplomatic Practice in the Middle Ages* (Hambledon and London 2003), 40–41.

5
Manuscript signatures

Although politicians enact statutes with a view to regulating human affairs, human ingenuity always manages to circumvent procedures and rules laid down in an attempt to provide for certainty. As a result, judges have been required to exercise their powers to test the definition of a signature, and what is acceptable in the legal context. The case law illustrates that, in general, judges assessed the validity of a signature in relation to the functions it performed. Different factual problems required a broader understanding of these functions. Whatever form a signature took, judges looked to the intent behind the use of the signature. Thus the range of forms a signature can take is wide, as demonstrated by the discussion in this and subsequent chapters.

In England, an early record of a manuscript signature is that of Edward III of 1362, who signed a document with his name. It is suggested it was already the custom to do this in Castile, and because he was writing to the king of Castile, he also appended his manuscript signature. The manuscript signature acted to confirm his recognition of the contents of the document, but not to replace the seal.[1]

Impression of a mark

A mark can be in the form of any shape, including the sign of the cross, an 'x', a shape or a number of lines that intersect.[2] One example is the mark on a memorandum dated 16 October 1666 of words spoken by Elizabeth Daniel of Eyam in the County of Derby as her last will and testament. Rebecca Hawksworth appended her mark on the memorandum as a witness to what was spoken and written down. Probate was granted on 24 April 1667. The mark consists of an incomplete line that is roughly in the shape of a heart, intersected with a further horizontal line.[3]

Bills of exchange

A case dating from 1798 is that of *Adam v Kerr*,[4] concerning a mark on a bill of exchange and whether the particular mark used by custom in Jamaica was acceptable as a valid signature. In 1830 the case of *George v Surrey*[5] dealt with the validity of a bill of exchange

---

1   Harvey and McGuinness, *Guide to British Medieval Seals*, 2 and n. 2.
2   Or a totemic signature: J. Walter Fewkes, 'Tusayan totemic signatures' (1897) 10(1) The American Anthropologist 1; also a pictogram, such as that of Massasoit on a land deed dated 1657 held at the Plymouth County Commissioners Office, Plymouth, Massachusetts, illustrated in Nathaniel Philbrick, *Mayflower A Voyage to War* (HarperPress 2006), 195.
3   A copy of this document is on display in the museum at Eyam, England, together with another document with the marks of three men; each of these marks is different in shape.
4   (1798) 1 B & P 360, 126 ER 952.
5   (1830) 1 M. & M. 516, 173 ER 1243.

in which Tindal CJ accepted a bill with a mark which included the endorsement 'Ann Moore her mark'.[6]

An interest in real property

In respect of the transfer of property, in the United States case of *Mitchell v Mills*,[7] a general warranty deed conveying property and signed by affixing a mark to the document before a notary public and witnesses was a sufficient signature, as was the sale of an erf (plot of land) in South Africa, where the mark was considered an act of the signer and signified assent to the content of the document.[8]

Wills

Before the majority of people could read and write, the provisions of some statutes meant that where a person could not write their name, they were still required to provide a mark on a will,[9] even when the will was signed with a signature but the codicil was signed by a mark,[10] and also where the will was signed by a mark where the testator was able to write.[11] This also applied to a witness,[12] and where a witness signed a will by marking the document with a cross.[13] Where an interested person added a mark to a will, the presumption was that the will was not valid.[14] The act

---

6   In the South African case of *Hanse v Jordan and Fuchs* 1909 19 CTR 530, the sum of £21 4s was due on a promissory note. The defendant claimed not to have added his mark. The magistrate at first instance, having heard the case, believed the plaintiff's account of the facts. On appeal, Buchanan J commented, at 530, 'The defendant denied this [adding his mark to the note], but the mere fact that he can write, and only signed by his mark, is not sufficient ground upon which the Court can upset the finding of the Magistrate upon the fact.'
7   264 S.E.2d 749 (1954).
8   *Chisnall and Chisnall v Sturgeon and Sturgeon* 1993 (2) SA 642 (W). For Scotland, see M. C. Meston and D. J. Cusine, 'Execution of deeds by a mark' (1993) Journal of the Law Society of Scotland 270.
9   In the case of *Crosbie v Wilson* (1865) 3 M. 870 in Scotland, a will was attested but had the testator's name at the end in words only with the statement 'her mark'. This was held to be ineffective as a signature.
10 *Baker v Dening* (1838) 8 AD & E 94, 112 ER 771; Patterson J indicated that when a document is signed by a mark, an enquiry may be undertaken as to the circumstances of the signing to ensure a will was properly attested. See also *Re Field's Goods* (1843) 3 Curt 752, 163 ER 890, although note *Hindmarch v Charlton* (1861) 8 HL Cas 160 and *Re Holtam, Gillett v Rogers* (1913) 108 LT 732.
11 *Taylor v Denning* (1838) 3 Nev. & P. 228, where the illness from which the testator was suffering made it difficult to write. In the 1929 New York case of *In the Matter of the Estate of Stegman*, 133 Misc. 745, 234 N.Y.S. 239, probate was denied where a testator, who was able to write, subscribed a third will with a mark. The proponent failed to prove the third and final will was valid. Evans S indicated, at 747, 'This manner of execution is not rare but it is unusual, for a person to sign by a mark that is able to write. This fact in itself does not invalidate a will but it is obvious that it calls for greater scrutiny on the part of the court.' For a contrary decision in Wisconsin in 1925, see *In re Mueller's Will*, 188 Wis. 183, 205 N.W. 814, 42 A.L.R. 951, where the testator made her mark even though she could write, and where a witness added the words 'her' above and 'mark' below the cross.
12 *Harrison v Harrison* (1803) 8 Ves Jun 185; 32 ER 324.
13 A will was held to be sufficiently signed where a testatrix signed with a mark without her name appearing on the document in *Re Bryce's Goods* (1839) 2 Curt 325, 163 ER 427.
14 *Paske v Ollat* (1815) 2 Phill 323, 161 ER 1158.

itself was not invalid, but strict proof was required, as noted by Lord Watson in the case of *Donnelly v Broughton*,[15] where he pointed out, at 442, that 'the onus of proof may be increased by circumstances, such as unbounded confidence in the drawer of the will, extreme debility in the testator, clandestinity and other circumstances which may increase the presumption even so much as to be conclusive against the instrument'.

United States of America

In the United States, the case law has covered a wider range of examples where judges have been required to determine the legal implications of various forms of mark and other signs, including fingerprints and an account number. A mark on a bill has been held sufficient as a means of authentication,[16] as it has on deeds,[17] insurance documents[18] and notices of appeal,[19] including in the form of a fingerprint,[20] under

---

15 [1891] AC 435 PC.

16 Federal: *Zacharie v Franklin*, 37 U.S. 151, 12 Pet. 151, 1838 WL 3945 (U.S.La.), 9 L.Ed. 1035 (the mark of Joseph Milah in a bill of sale comprising slaves, their children, and stock and household furniture had the same effect as a signature) (1838).

Indiana (1867): *Shank v Butsch*, 28 Ind. 19, 1867 WL 2925 (Ind.).

New Hampshire: *Willoughby v Moulton*, 47 N.H. 205, 1866 WL 1982 (N.H.) (a promissory note signed by a mark may be valid against the person signing, even though there was no subscribing witness).

New York: *Brown v The Butchers & Drovers' Bank*, 6 Hill 443, 41 Am.Dec. 755 (a person writing '1. 2. 8.' on the back of a bill of exchange as a substitute for his name served to endorse the bill) (1844).

Tennessee: *Brown v McClanahan*, 68 Tenn. 347, 1878 WL 4292 (Tenn.), 9 Baxt. 347, 2 Leg.Rep. 59.

South Carolina: *Zimmerman v Sale*, 37 S.C.L. 76, 3 Rich. 76, 1846 WL 2269 (S.C.App.L.) (a mark that was not accompanied by the name of the person making the mark remains a signature) (1864).

17 Carolina (1891): *Devereux v McMahon*, 108 N.C. 134, 12 S.E. 902, 12 L.R.A. 205.

Kentucky: *Blair v Campbell*, 45 S.W. 93, 19 Ky.L.Rptr. 2012 (a deed signed with a mark and acknowledged before the county clerk was held to be sufficient as a signature) (1898); *Stephens v Perkins*, 273 S.W. 545 (in the conveyance of property, the marks of nine heirs were sufficient as signature of the conveyance) (1925).

Georgia: *Horton v Murden*, 117 Ga. 72, 43 S.E. 786 (a deed signed 'I, J. R., sign my hand to it X here' was sufficiently signed) (1903).

18 Georgia: *Thurmond v Spoon*, 125 Ga.App. 811, 189 S.E.2d 92 (a mark affixed to a beneficiary card was a sufficient signature) (1972). Dissenting, Evans J articulated the view that the name of the person must be affixed to the document as well as a mark.

Pennsylvania: *Tomilio v Pisco*, 123 Pa. Super. 423, 187 A. 86 (it was a signature where the person signing was too weak to sign their name, but made an undecipherable series of curves and strokes) (1936).

19 North Carolina: *State v Byrd*, 93 N.C. 624, 1885 WL 1753 (N.C.).

Wisconsin: *Finley v Prescott*, 47 L.R.A. 695, 104 Wis. 614, 80 N.W. 930 (appeal papers may be signed by a mark, and there was no statutory requirement to have the signature of a person in the form of a mark witnessed) (1899).

20 Illinois: *Matter of the Estate of Deskovic*, 21 Ill.App.2d 209, 157 N.E.2d 769, 72 A.L.R.2d 1261 (1st Dist. 1959).

New York (1937): *In the Matter of the Estate of Romaniw*, 163 Misc. 481, 296 N.Y.S. 925.

the relevant Statute of Frauds (including a trade mark),[21] with respect to trover and conversion,[22] and wills.[23]

Illegible writing

It is rare for illegible writing to be the subject of legal proceedings, although in 1862 the surname on a notice of objection was disputed because it was not legible.[24] The appeal court reversed the decision of the revising barrister, and held that the notice of objection was sufficient. Earle CJ observed, at 39:

> Lastly, it is one thing to say that the statute enjoins a legible signature, and another thing to say that such legibility is a condition precedent to the validity of the notice. Were we to hold this notice bad, questions would arise on the notice or claim of every man who might have written his name very badly or spelt it incorrectly. The object of the act of parliament, which calls to its aid persons of

---

21   Federal: *Bibb v Allen*, 149 U.S. 481, 13 S.Ct. 950, 37 L.Ed. 819, 50 L.R.A. 240 (telegrams containing orders in the form of Shepperton's Code, and which directed the sales delivery for accounts of designated names, such as 'Albert', 'Alfred', 'Alexander', 'Amanda', 'Andrew' and 'Winston', were intended and understood to represent the firm name of B. S. Bibb & Co. and held to be sufficient as a signature) (1893); Federal 4th circuit: *Barber & Ross Co. v Lifetime Doors, Inc.*, 810 F.2d 1276 (4th Cir. 1987), 3 U.C.C. Rep.Serv.2d (CBC) 41 (a trademark printed on a written sales brochure met the requirements of the Statute of Frauds and signature requirement).

Missouri: *Defur v Westinghouse Electric Corporation*, 677 F.Supp. 622 (E.D.Mo. 1988) (writings with the defendant's trademark printed on them constituted signed writings).

22   Massachusetts: *Foye v Patch*, 132 Mass. 105, 1882 WL 10891 (Mass.) (adding a mark to a written agreement was a satisfactory signature).

23   Illinois: *Cunningham v Hallyburton*, 342 Ill. 442, 174 N.E. 420 (1930); *In re Westerman's Will*, 401 Ill. 489, 82 N.E.2d 474 (1948) (the will of Minnie Westerman (her maiden name) dated 13 April 1942 revoked an earlier will dated 9 April 1942 and executed under her married name of Wilhelmina Frederichs, when both wills were signed with her mark, notwithstanding she was not authorized to resume using her maiden name in her second divorce proceedings).

New York: 1809 case of *Jackson v Van Dusen*, 5 Johns 144; 1847 case of *Butler v Benson*, 1 Barb. 533; *Jackson v Jackson*, 39 N.Y. 153, 12 Tiffany 153, 1868 WL 6249 (N.Y.) (after trying for some time to apply the pen to the paper to sign his name, the hand of the deceased trembled so much that he made a cross on his will); *In the Matter of the Estate of Galvin*, 78 Misc.2d 22, 355 N.Y.2d 751 (a mark added to a will by the daughter and at the request of the deceased was a valid signature of the deceased) (1974).

Pennsylvania: *Main v Ryder*, 84 Pa. 217, 4 W.N.C. 173, 1877 WL 13243 (Pa.) (signing a will with a mark while touching the writing instrument held and controlled by another person) (1877). Note: in Pennsylvania, a new Act was enacted in 1833 requiring the manuscript signature of a testator, and a mark was no longer permitted, for which see *Assay v Hoover*, 5 Pa. St. 21 (1846); *Grabill v Barr*, 5 Pa. 441, 5 Barr. 441, 1846 WL 5049 (Pa.), 47 Am.Dec. 418; but see *Long v Zook*, 13 Pa. 400, 1850 WL 5764 (Pa.), 1 Harris 400 where Gibson CJ, in applying the revised Act of 1848, commented that the 1833 Act probably defeated more true wills than false ones; also note the comments of Gibson CJ in the earlier case of *Greenough v Greenough*, 11 Pa.St. 497, 1849 WL 5732 (Pa.).

Texas: 1934 case of *Short v Short*, 67 S.W.2d 425; 1937 case of *Mortgage Bond Corporation v Haney*, 105 S.W.2d 488.

Virginia: *Clarke v Dunnavant*, 10 Leigh 13, 37 Va. 13 (1839).

Wisconsin: *Will of Susan Jenkins*, 43 Wis. 610, 1878 WL 3217 (Wis.).

24   *Trotter v Walker* (1862) 13 CB (NS) 29, 143 ER 12.

very imperfect education, might be defeated by adopting a rigorous construction, and furthered by a more benignant one.

In Scotland, an illegible signature by the testator on a codicil was accepted as a signature in *Stirling Stuart v Stirling Crawfurd's Trustees*.[25] In this case, Mr Crawfurd was not able to write, not even his own name, without becoming affected with a tremor, which meant that his writing was shaky and irregular. The Lord President made an interesting observation at 625–626 on the issue of illegible writing:

> it is said that if you examine this particular signature without reference to any other signature of the testator, it is utterly illegible, and that the Court is not entitled to give effect to an illegible signature. That proposition is stated a great deal too broadly. Illegible signatures are not uncommon even when the writer is not suffering from the infirmity under which Mr Crawfurd suffered, but from other infirmities altogether. The infirmity of affectation is perhaps, of all others, most productive of illegible signatures. Many persons of the highest ability and skill in penmanship sign in such a manner that it is impossible for anyone seeing their signatures for the first time to say what is meant by them. Now, are all those illegible signatures to be disregarded? I think that a very dangerous doctrine, and I am not prepared to accede to it. Does it then make any difference if the illegibility arises from an infirmity such as Mr Crawfurd suffered from? I think not. If it is clear that this is written by him, and if it is made out that that is the kind of writing by which he was in the habit of representing his name in deeds, how does the case differ from illegibility arising from other causes? You require evidence in both instances to enable you to say what the writing is; here you require someone to tell you that what is written stands for 'William Stuart Stirling Crawfurd', while in the other cases I have referred to you require to be instructed that that is the ordinary way in which the writer signs his name.

In Ireland, two scrawls that were undecipherable but intended to be initials were accepted as a mark under the Wills Act 1837,[26] and in Canada it was held that a manuscript signature of a justice of the peace does not render the information invalid if it is not legible, because of the presumption of regularity.[27] In the United States, judges have also been required to consider illegible scrawl,[28] and in the 1890 Pennsylvanian case of *Appeal of Knox*[29] it was held that a note written by the deceased and signed with her first name 'Harriet' was a signature. Mitchell J remarked, at 1023, that 'Custom controls the rule of names, and so it does the rule of signature'. He went on to note, in relation to the difficulty in reading a signature:

> So the form which a man customarily uses to identify and bind himself in writing is his signature, whatever shape he may choose to give it. There is no requirement that it shall be legible, though legibility is one of the prime objects of writing. It is sufficient if it be such as he usually signs, and the signatures of neither Rufus Choate nor General Spinner could be rejected, though no man, unaided, could discover what the ragged marks made by either of those two eminent personages were intended to represent. Nor is there any fixed requirement how much of

---

25 (1885) 12 R. 610.
26 *In the Goods of Kiernan, deceased* [1933] IR 222.
27 *R v Kapoor*, 52 CCC (3d) 41.
28 Alabama: *Dew v Garner*, 7 Port. 503, 1838 WL 1335 (Ala.); Mississippi (1896): *Sheehan v Kearney*, 82 Miss. 688, 21 So. 41, 35 L.R.A. 102; Pennsylvania (1936): *Tomilio v Pisco*, 123 Pa. Super. 423, 187 A. 86; Wyoming (1929): *In re Iverson's Estate*, 39 Wyo. 482, 273 P. 684, 64 A.L.R. 203.
29 131 P. 220, 18 A. 1021, 6 L.R.A. 353, 17 Am.St.Rep. 798.

the full name shall be written. Custom varies with time and place, and habit with the whim of the individual. Sovereigns write only their first names, and the sovereign of Spain, more royally still, signs his decrees only, 'I, the King' (Yo el Rey). English peers now sign their titles only, though they be geographical names, like Devon or Stafford, as broad as a county. The great Bacon wrote his name 'Fr. Verulam', and the ordinary signature of the poet-philosopher of fishermen was 'Iz: Wa'. In the fifty-six signatures to the most solemn instrument of modern times, the Declaration of Independence, we find every variety from Th. Jefferson to the unmistakably identified Charles Carroll, of Carrollton. In the present day it is not uncommon for business men to have a signature for checks and banking purposes somewhat different from that used in their ordinary business, and, in familiar correspondence, signature by initials or nickname or diminutive is probably the general practice.[30]

In South Africa, Murray J concluded in the case of *Van Niekerk v Smit*[31] that a letter on headed notepaper with the name and address of the firm was properly signed, even though indecipherable marks were made with a lead pencil, perhaps representing initials, over the concluding words in type 'Ferreira en van Zyl'. In *SAI Investments v Vander Schyff NO*[32] it was held that extrinsic evidence was admissible to indicate the identity of an illegible signature on the agreement where the signature of the person signing as purchaser on the last page was indecipherable, as were the names of the two witnesses who attested to the signature. A similar finding was made on appeal in the case of *Van der Merwe v Kenkes (Edms) BPK*,[33] where the appellant was clearly identified in an agreement as the purchaser, but the signatures of both the purchaser and the seller were illegible. Extrinsic evidence to indicate that the illegible signature was that of the appellant or her husband was admissible.

Assisted signature or mark

The problems associated with people who are too ill or too weak to sign a document are well illustrated in the South African case of *Matanda v Rex*,[34] where a boy of thirteen could not write. He made a statement to a magistrate, described at 436:

> My practice, which we adopted in this case, is for the witness to come up to me, I hand the pen to him, he touches the pen and then I make the mark for him. I hold one end of the pen and he holds the other, after he is told to what he is deposing. He is not actually holding the pen at one end while I am making the mark. I hand him the pen, holding it myself. He fingers it. Then I take it and I make the mark. That is what happened in this case.

A similar point was discussed in *Fulton v Kee*,[35] where the members of the Court of Appeal distinguished between a will signed by the testator with assistance or by direction. In the 1975 New York case of *In re Estate of McCready*[36] and the 1927

---

30 Note his comments at 1022 about *Vernon v Kirk*, 30 Pa.St. 222 (1858); *Assay v Hoover*, 5 Pa. St. 21 and *Grabill v Barr*, 5 Pa. 441, 5 Barr. 441, 1846 WL 5049 (Pa.), 47 Am.Dec. 418 and the subsequent change of the law.
31 1952 (3) SA 17 (T).
32 1999 (3) SA 340 (N).
33 1983 (3) SA 909 (T).
34 1923 AD 435 (B).
35 [1961] NI 1, CA (NI).
36 369 N.Y.S.2d 325, 82 Misc.2d 531.

Pennsylvania case of *Brehony v Brehony*,[37] the mark of a person who was blind that was made with the assistance of another was considered a signature.

Wills

Where a person is too ill to sign a document, one question might be whether there is any evidence to demonstrate the person intended to sign. In the case of *Wilson v Beddard*,[38] the testator made a will dated 7 September 1826 and died the following day. The will was signed by the testator's mark, his hand being guided by another person. Before making the mark, the testator made faint strokes on each of the sheets containing the will. On the motion for a new trial, the Vice-Chancellor, Sir L Shadwell, agreed with the trial judge, Parke B, that the will was signed by the testator. It was decided that the act of making the faint strokes provided evidence that the testator intended to sign the will, and the fact that he was helped by another person to place his mark on the document did not make the mark any less of a signature.

A name without a signature

There are occasions when a person makes a promise that they later refuse to fulfil for some reason. Such was the case in *Knight v Crockford*,[39] where Crockford agreed to sell a public house to Knight. Given the evidence in this case, Eyre CJ determined that the draft agreement was a sufficient agreement, and although only Knight had affixed his signature to the document, the words 'I, James Crockford, agree to sell, &c' written by Crockford were considered a signature within the meaning of the Statute of Frauds 1677.

Mistake as to the name

Sometimes humans make mistakes, and in circumstances where the better response is to render an equitable result, judges have, on occasion, disregarded minor issues in respect to wills. For instance, in *Re Clarke's Goods*[40] the testatrix was described as 'Susannah Clarke', and executed the will with a mark, against which was written 'Susannah Barrell, her mark', Barrell having been her maiden name. Sir C. Cresswell was satisfied that the mark was that of Susannah Clarke, and thought the additional words next to the mark did not matter.[41]

---

37 289 Pa. 267, 137 A. 260.
38 (1841) 12 Sim 28, 59 ER 1041.
39 (1794) 1 Esp 190, 170 ER 324; the insertion of names into a document that the parties intended to sign did not equate to the document being signed: *Hubert v Treherne* (1842) 3 Man. & G. 743, 133 ER 1338.
40 (1858) LJR 27 NS P & M 18, 1 Sw & Tr 22; 164 ER 611.
41 *Re Douce's Goods* (1862) 2 Sw & Tr 592, 164 ER 1127 where the deceased was mistakenly described as John Douce, but his name was actually Thomas Douce. This case was considered in the New Zealand case of *In re McNamee* (1912) 31 NZLR 1007, where the deceased executed a will giving all his property to his wife, then executed a second will giving all his property to his wife, but in the blank space for his name he merely inserted a cross for his name. Williams J concluded that there was sufficient proof to grant letters of administration, given that there was an affidavit by the witness to the execution of the will, and the name of his wife appeared in both wills.

Variations of a name

Voting

Administrative mistakes tend not to be considered an adequate reason for preventing people from casting their vote. In *R v Thwaites*[42] the names of a number of men entitled to vote were listed on the burgess roll incorrectly. When they voted, they signed the voting papers with their correct names. It was held that the men had a right to vote, and although they voted with different names in comparison to the names listed on the roll, they were the men mentioned in the burgess roll and this was a mere case of misnomer within the provisions of s142 of the Municipal Corporation Act of 5 & 6 Will. 4 c76 1853.

Wills

There are times when some people will adopt alternative names for a variety of reasons. For instance, they may forget to write their present name, as in the case of *In the Goods of Glover*,[43] where a woman signed her will with the name of her first husband, 'Susan Reeve', and then placed the will into an envelope marked by her 'The will of Susan Glover'. Alternatively, a person might use a substitute name.[44] In Scotland, a letter written and sent from one sister to another was capable of constituting a holographic will, and the subscription of her Christian name 'Connie' was also a sufficient authentication.[45]

United States of America

A range of variations of a name have been tested in the United States courts, including the use of a fictitious name on deeds,[46] and using the name of another without permission on a promissory note.[47] More commonly, mistaken or partial names have appeared in matters relating to a lien,[48] the Statute of Frauds,[49]

---

42   (1853) 22 LJQB 238.
43   (1847) 11 Jur. 1022, 5 Notes of Cases 553.
44   *Re Reddings Goods* (1850) 14 Jur 1052, 2 Rob Ecc 338, 163 ER 1338. The two law reports differ as to whether the testatrix signed her first name with the initial 'C' or 'Charlotte'.
45   *Draper v Thomason* 1954 SC 136, 1954 SLT 222.
46   Arkansas (1947): *Walker v Emrich*, 212 Ark. 598, 206 S.W.2d 769.
New York: *David v Williamsburgh City Fire Insurance Company*, 83 N.Y. 265, 38 Sickels 265, 1880 WL 12653 (N.Y.), 38 Am.Rep. 418 (where a person adopted a fictitious name with intent to convey title, he was bound by the name he adopted when executing a conveyance of the property).
47   New Hampshire: *Grafton Bank v Flanders*, 4 N.H. 239, 1827 WL 744 (N.H.) (a person putting the name of another on a promissory note without authority from any person of that name was liable for the note).
48   Federal 2nd circuit: *In the Matter of Excel Stores, Inc.*, 341 F.2d 961 (1965) (use of the name 'Excel Department Stores' instead of the correct name 'Excel Stores, Inc' was a minor error and not seriously misleading when the contract was properly signed by an appropriate officer of the company).
49   Massachusetts: *Fessenden v Mussey*, 65 Mass. 127, 1853 WL 4969 (Mass.) (the name 'Benj. Mussey' as recorded at the time of the auction was held to be a signature, even though it omitted the middle letter of the defendant's name); *Walker v Walker*, 175 Mass. 349, 56 N.E. 601 (a marriage contract was deemed to be signed where the defendant signed the document with her first name only) (1900).
Missouri: *Great Western Printing Co. v Belcher*, 127 Mo.App. 133, 104 S.W. 894 (the words 'Guaranteed. Belcher' written in lead pencil across the face of the original account was a signature, even though the signature did not include the first name) (1907).

mortgages,[50] the name of a partnership on an arbitration bond[51] and on a writ,[52] and it is not surprising that the range of human behaviour is more widely reflected in the cases of wills,[53] although the liberal approach in extending the meaning of a signature was not applied to the 1914 Pennsylvanian case of *In re Brennan's Estate*,[54] where a testamentary paper ending with 'your miserable father' was held not to have been executed correctly.

The use of initials
Statute of Frauds

The use of initials has been held sufficient to be a mark or signature to indicate the intent of a party under the provisions of the Statute of Frauds, as in the case of *Phillimore v Barry*.[55] Messrs Fector and Minet of Dover stored a quantity of rum, the cargo of a Danish prize, which was to be sold by auction in various lots on 28 April 1808. Before the day of the sale, the defendants wrote to Fector and Minet asking them to buy thirteen puncheons of the rum. As a result, Mr John Minet Fector of the firm bid for several lots, which were duly knocked down to him. The auctioneer wrote down in the printed catalogue the initials 'I.M.F.' opposite each lot sold to the defendant. On 11 May 1808 the defendants subsequently wrote a letter to Fector and Minet, recognizing and approving the purchase. The warehouse accidentally caught fire on 18 May 1808, and a quantity of gunpowder stored in the building exploded (that is, it burnt rapidly at a subsonic speed), destroying the rum. There was no evidence that a deposit had been paid. The defendants claimed the contract was void under the Statute of Frauds on the basis that there was no memorandum in writing. It was also submitted that the auctioneer was not the authorized agent of the defendants, and even if he were, the inclusion of the initials against each lot could not be considered a memorandum of agreement. It was also contended that the rum remained at the risk of the sellers for thirty days, and the property did not vest with the defendant.

Lord Ellenborough held that Mr Minet was the agent to the defendants, and that his initials as written by the auctioneer in the catalogue, together with the defendant's letter confirming the sale, constituted a sufficient memorandum in writing to satisfy the Statute of Frauds. He also held that the property vested absolutely in the purchasers from the moment of sale, and the provision of storage for thirty days was part of the consideration for which the purchase money was to be paid. While the finding by

---

50 California: *Middleton v Findla*, 25 Cal. 76, 1864 WL 629 (Cal.) (a grantor who signed a deed using an incorrect name (Edmund Jones) with his correct name in the body of the deed (Edward Jones) did not invalidate the conveyance).

Indiana: *Zann v Haller*, 71 Ind. 136, 1880 WL 6236 (Ind.), 23 Am.Rep. 193 (a woman signing a mortgage deed with her first name only was accepted as a signature).

51 New York: *Mackay v J. and L. Bloodgood*, 9 Johns. 285 (the affixing of the name and seal of a firm by one partner bound the other partner) (1812).

52 Maine: *Sawtelle v Wardwell*, 56 Me. 146, 1868 WL 1770 (Me.) (the surname of an attorney on the back of a writ of endorsement was a sufficient signature), although note the dissenting judgment of Kent J.

53 Kentucky: *Wells v Lewis*, 190 Ky. 626, 228 S.W. 3 (the signature 'Ant Nanie' appended to a letter as a testamentary writing was a sufficient signature) (1921).

54 91 A. 220, 244 Pa. 574.

55 (1808) 1 Camp 513, 170 ER 1040.

Lord Ellenborough was not relevant to whether the initials represented a signature, nevertheless they were considered part of the evidence to demonstrate that a contract existed between the parties.

In *Chichester v Cobb*,[56] the defendant wrote a letter to Mary Ann Williams, as follows:

> Kensington, 21st July 1865
>
> My dear M. A. – So soon as all pecuniary and necessary arrangements are made to constitute an unquestionable legal marriage as proposed, I will be prepared to pay over for your behalf 300*l*., and concur in every practicable measure by which an equitable share, or its equivalent, in the settled property can be assured to you. I shall expect to see Edward here this evening, as requested in my note to him of last evening. – Yours ever affectionately, E.C.

After the marriage, the defendant refused to pay the £300. Blackburn and Shee JJ in the Queen's Bench agreed that the initials constituted a sufficient signing of the contract or memorandum to satisfy the Statute of Frauds.

Judicial use

There is a case where a judge in England and Wales signed a bill of indictment with his initials. In *R v Morais (Carlton)*,[57] a bill of indictment was signed in manuscript 'Cor. The Honourable Mr. Justice Roch' and underneath, in the judge's handwriting, the words 'Leave to prefer' and his initials, 'J. R.', with the date '23.9.87' and the words 'A Justice of the High Court'. This form of signature was held not to be a signature by Lord Lane CJ in the Court of Appeal. A new trial was ordered.[58]

Judicial officers in the United States have used initials, although the decisions do not always indicate approval of the use of initials in the absence of a full signature.[59] In the 1933 Federal case of *George A. Ohl & Co. v A. L. Smith Iron Works*,[60] the use of a judge's initials followed by 'D. J.' was held as a signature authenticating a bill of exceptions, and the initials 'D. J.' were added for the purpose of indicating his judicial office. Hughes CJ commented on the use of initials at 176–177:

---

56 (1866) 14 LTNS 433.
57 [1988] 3 All ER 161, [1988] 3 WLUK 82, (1988) 87 Cr App R 9, (1988) 152 JP 355, [1988] Crim LR 459, (1988) 152 JPN 383, [1988] CLY 654.
58 Surprisingly, no case law on signatures appears to have been cited or referred to in the appeal, which is particularly interesting bearing in mind the comments by Buxton and Brooke LJJ in *Copeland v Smith* [2000] 1 WLR 1371, [2000] 1 All ER 457, [1999] 10 WLUK 381, (1999) 143 SJLB 276, Times, 20 October 1999, [1999] CLY 457.
59 Federal: *Origet v United States*, 125 U.S. 240, 8 S.Ct. 846, 31 L.Ed. 743 (the initials 'A.B.' were held not to be a signature of the judge, nor sufficient authentication of a bill of exceptions) (1888); *Kinney v United States Fidelity & Guaranty Company*, 222 U.S. 283, 32 S.Ct. 101, 56 L.Ed. 200 (a paper in the record styled 'Exceptions to the Charge to the Jury' upon which the initials 'J. P. McP., Trial Judge' were placed was not a bill of exceptions) (1911).

Kentucky: *Wurts v Newsome*, 253 Ky. 38, 68 S.W.2d 448 (there was no signature where a judge signed a ballot with his surname and initial, or with his initials) (1934).
60 288 U.S. 170, 53 S.Ct. 340, 77 L.Ed. 681.

Signature by initials has been held to be sufficient under the Statute of Frauds and the Statute of Wills, and in other transactions. It has been held in some states that a different rule obtains in the case of the official signature of certain judicial officers, but the Congress has not established such a rule for the judges of the federal courts. Nor, in the absence of special statutory requirement, is there a uniform custom in relation to official signatures. It may be assumed that a requirement of the officer's signature, without more, means that he shall write his name or his distinctive appellation; but the question remains as to what writing of that character is to be deemed sufficient for the purpose of authenticating his official act. There is no rule that he shall adhere to the precise form of his name as it appears in his commission. The full name of the officer may or may not be used. Not infrequently Christian names are omitted, in part or altogether, or are abbreviated or indicated by initials. In some of the most important communications on behalf of the federal government, only the surname of the officer is used. When an officer authenticates his official act by affixing his initials he does not entirely omit to use his name; he simply abbreviates it; he uses a combination of letters which are part of it. Undoubtedly that method is informal, but we think that it is clearly a method of 'signing'. It cannot be said in such a case that he has utterly failed to 'sign', so that his authentication of his official act, in the absence of further statutory requirement, is to be regarded as absolutely void.

The cases of *Origet v United States*[61] and *Kinney v United States Fidelity & Guaranty Company*[62] were neither cited nor referred to as being overruled, although the comments by Hughes CJ appear to indicate that initials are acceptable. The initials of a judge on a judgment were held to be sufficient in the Illinois case of *Robertson v Robertson*,[63] and in the 1905 Nebraska case of *Griffith v Bonawitz*[64] the initials of two judges, written on the back of a number of ballots, were also held to be signatures.

Wills

Initials have been used in wills, as in the case of *Re Savory's Goods*[65] where the testatrix executed the will by writing her initials in the presence of two witnesses who duly attested.[66] See also *In the Goods of Clark*,[67] where the deceased, who was too ill to sign his will, requested his wife to sign for him, which she did, with her mark. This was a sufficient compliance with the Act, although the executrix lost a legacy that was granted to her under the terms of the will. In the case of *In the Goods of Christian*,[68] H. H. Christian, a rear admiral in the Royal Navy, left a will that included the signature of a witness in the form of initials, which was also a sufficient subscription. For a line of

---

61 125 U.S. 240, 8 S.Ct. 846, 31 L.Ed. 743 (1888).
62 222 U.S. 283, 32 S.Ct. 101, 56 L.Ed. 200 (1911).
63 462 N.E.2d 712 (Ill.App. 5 Dist. 1984).
64 73 Neb. 622, 103 N.W. 327 (1905).
65 (1856) 15 Jur 1042.
66 In Scotland initials were not accepted in the case of a witness initialling a will in the case of *Meek v Dunlop* [1707] Mor 16806.
67 (1839) 2 Curt. 329, 163 ER 428.
68 (1849) 2 Rob. Ecc. 110, 163 ER 1260.

cases in England with respect to wills, see *Re Blewitt's Goods*,[69] and in Scotland, initials were considered a form of signature in *Speirs v Speirs or Home Speirs*.[70]

In South Africa, a will signed with initials was considered signed in the case of *In re Trollip*,[71] in which the decision in *Van Vuuren v Van Vuuren*[72] was overruled and the decision in the case of *In re Ebden's Will*[73] approved. De Villiers CJ observed, at 245, that 'If a mark is a sufficient signature, *a fortiori* initials must be sufficient'. A modern example of a will in which initials were accepted as sufficient evidence of a signature is the Canadian case of *Re Schultz*.[74]

Rights in property

In respect of rights in property, the initials of a landlord in a rent book served to renew a lease and enable an option to buy to be exercised,[75] and directors adding their initials to a clause providing a guarantee in a contract were bound by the guarantee under the provisions of s2 of the Contracts Enforcement Act 1956 in the New Zealand case of *Doughty-Pratt Group Limited v Perry Castle*.[76] Although it was accepted that initials can be considered a signature in *Newell v Tarrant*,[77] in the particular circumstances of that case the initials in question did not amount to an execution and authentication to create an equitable charge over Chase Farm, and the initials also failed to comply with the strict requirements of s2(3) of the Law of Property (Miscellaneous Provisions) Act 1989.[78]

Voting

In the nineteenth century voting papers had to be signed with the name of the burgess voting under the provisions of s32 of the Municipal Corporation Act 1853. In 1852, in the case of *R v Avery*,[79] it was held that a person could sign as they ordinarily write their signature, such as, in this instance, the surname and initial of the Christian name.

Human Fertilisation and Embryology Act 1990

Schedule 3, para 1(1) requires that 'A consent under this Schedule, and any notice under paragraph 4 varying or withdrawing a consent under this Schedule, must be in writing and ... must be signed by the person giving it'. In *Jefferies v BMI Healthcare Ltd (Human Fertilisation and Embryology)*,[80] the question was whether initials constituted

---

69 (1879–81) 5 PD 116.
70 (1879) 6 R. 1359, although see *Meek v Dunlop* [1707] Mor 16806.
71 1895 12 SC 243.
72 (1855) 2 Searle 116.
73 (1885–86) 4 Juta 495.
74 (1984) 8 DLR (4th) 147.
75 *Hill v Hill* [1947] 1 Ch 231, [1947] 1 All ER 54, [1946] 12 WLUK 8, 176 LT 216, (1947) 91 SJ 55, [1947–51] CLY 5569.
76 [1995] 2 NZLR 398 (CA).
77 [2004] EWHC 772 (Ch), [2004] 4 WLUK 193, (2004) 148 SJLB 509.
78 For a similar decision in Scotland regarding the Conveyancing (Scotland) Act 1874, see *Gardner v Beresford's Trustees* [1878] SLR 15 359.
79 (1852) 21 LJQB 430.
80 [2016] EWHC 2493 (Fam), [2016] 10 WLUK 243, [2017] 2 FLR 664, [2016] Med LR 656, [2017] CLY 1141.

a signature. Sir James Munby P determined that initials are acceptable as a signature under the provisions of the schedule.

United States of America

In the United States, decisions relating to the use of initials covers a range of situations, including bills,[81] cheques (checks),[82] the Statute of Frauds,[83] trusts[84] and wills,[85] although the evidence does not always indicate that initials served as a means of authentication, as in the 1945 Wisconsin case of *North American Seed Co. v Cedarburg Supply Co.*,[86] where the initials 'H. Z.' for Harvey Zirtzlaff were placed in such an odd position that it was determined they did not serve as a signature. Attempts are made on occasions to retrieve a small scintilla of hope from an otherwise impossible position, which is what was attempted in the federal eighth circuit case of *Vess Beverages, Inc. v The Paddington Corporation*,[87] where the initials of those attending

---

81 New York (1845): *Palmer v Stevens*, 1 Denio 471.
82 New York: *The Merchants' Bank v Spicer*, 6 Wend. 443 (the initials of the defendant on a cheque was held to be a sufficient endorsement) (1831).
83 Federal: *The Salmon Falls Manufacturing Company v Goddard*, 55 U.S. 446, 14 How. 446, 1852 WL 6760 (U.S. Mass.), 14 L.Ed. 493 (the initials 'R.M.M.' and 'W.W.G.' were sufficient to be signatures) (1852); Federal 5th Circuit: *Jones v Fox Film Corporation*, 68 F.2d 116 (the initials 'J.T.J.' for John T. Jones were held to be a signature) (1934); Federal 7th Circuit: *Monetti, S.P.A. v Anchor Hocking Corporation*, 931 F.2d 1178 (7th Cir. 1991) (the initials 'SS/mh' typed by a secretary was held to be the signature of Steve Schneider, who dictated the letter to the secretary).

Iowa: *Burns v Burrows*, 196 N.W. 62, 196 Iowa 80 (the initials 'R.A.S.' were held to be a signature of R. A. Santee) (1923).

Massachusetts: *Irving v Goodimate, Co.*, 320 Mass. 454, 70 N.E.2d 414, 171 A.L.R. 326 (the initials 'RL/s' of the president of the company were typed at the bottom of a letter); *Sanborn v Flagler*, 9 Allen 474, 91 Mass. 474, 1864 WL 3510 (Mass.) (initials of both parties, 'J.H.F.' and 'J.B.R.', were signatures) (1946).

Michigan: *Archbold v Industrial Land Co.*, 264 Mich. 289, 249 N.W. 858 (an instrument signed 'Approved: J.S.L.' and 'O.K. with me: O.T.B.' and 'O.K. with me: O.T.M.' was held to be signed by O. G. Bowker and J. S. Lille, respectively president and vice-president of the Industrial Land company, and O. T. Morse, vice-president of the American Blower Corporation) (1933); *Borkowski v Kolodziejski*, 332 Mich. 589, 52 N.W.2d 348 (defendant signed his name with the initials 'L.S.' after it) (1952).

Missouri: *Kamada, M.D. v RX Group Limited*, 639 S.W.2d 146, (Mo.App. 1982) (initials on a lease sufficient).

New Jersey: *Smith v Howell*, 11 N.J.Eq. 349, 1857 WL 4462 (N.J.Ch.), 3 Stockt. 349 (the initials of Walter Kirkpatrick were used by him as his signature to form a trust) (1857); *Crabtree v Elizabeth Arden Sales Corporation*, 305 N.Y. 48, 110 N.E.2d 551 (the initials of Robert P. Johns, executive vice-president and general manager, subscribed to a payroll card was a signature for the purposes of establishing an employment contract) (1953).

Washington: *Degginger v Martin*, 48 Wash. 1, 92 P. 674 (the initials of an agent were added by him in his own hand underneath his typewritten name; the contract held to be sufficiently executed) (1907).

84 California: *Weiner v Mullaney*, 59 Cal.App.2d 620, 140 P.2d 704 (the initials of George J. Mullaney typed at the end of several letters to his sister comprised a signature sufficiently signed in the formation of a trust) (1943).
85 Virginia: *Pilcher v Pilcher*, 117 Va. 356, 84 S.E. 667, L.R.A. 1915D 902 (a will written by the testator in the form 'I give to my wife, Alice McCabe Pilcher, all of my property, real and personal. E.M.P.' was held to be sufficiently signed) (1915).
86 247 Wis. 31, 18 N.W.2d 466, 159 A.L.R. 250.
87 941 F.2d 651 (8th Cir. 1991).

a meeting that were added by the person who took a note of the meeting did not constitute individual signatures, and thus did not qualify as a means of authentication.

The use of a surname

Statute of Frauds

People use many variations of their name when signing a document, and the use of first name or family name is not unusual. In the context of the Statute of Frauds, the question about what could be construed as a signature was argued before Lord Denham CJ and Patteson, Coleridge and Wrightman JJ in the case of *Lobb and Knight v Stanley* in 1844.[88] Interestingly, the comments made both by counsel and Patteson J in this case seem to imply that contemporaries would have preferred to reverse the liberal approach relating to the meaning of a signature. However, the authorities were too well established to be reviewed or ignored. In this instance, one Stanley, a certified bankrupt, gave a written promise signed by him after his bankruptcy. Three undated letters were produced, one of which read:

> Mr Stanley begs to inform Mr Lobb that he will be glad to give him a promissory note or bill for the amount of Mr Stanley's account, payable at three months, as Mr Stanley has of late been put to heavy expenses, and hopes this arrangement will be satisfactory to Mr Lobb. 3 Crescent. Thursday morning.

At the trial before Lord Denman CJ, a verdict was found for Lobb, and leave was given to appeal. Whately, counsel for Stanley, submitted that all the previous decisions relating to what was meant to be a signature were not correct. He argued: 'Those decisions, however, are scarcely to be defended on principle; and, if the question were new, probably a different doctrine would be adopted.'[89] This view was noted and commented upon by Patteson J:

> It is true that the word 'signed' occurs in the statute: and, if this had been the first time that we were called upon to put a construction on that word, and if the decisions on the Statute of Frauds had not occurred, I should perhaps be slow to say that this was a signature.[90]

Lord Denham CJ agreed that in one sense the letters were not signed. However, he then considered the intrinsic evidence of the documents, and pointed out that:

> it is a signature of the party when he authenticates the instrument by writing his name in the body. Here, it is true, the whole name is not written, but only 'Mr Stanley'. I think more is not necessary.[91]

Coleridge J reinforced the significance of the mechanism by which the document was authenticated when he pointed out that:

> Is it not enough if a party, at the beginning of a document, writes his name so as to govern what follows? Does he not then use his name as a signature?[92]

---

88 (1844) 5 QB 574, 114 ER 1366, Law Times, 2 (1843–44) Law Times (2), 366.
89 (1844) 5 QB 574 at 579.
90 (1844) 5 QB 574 at 582.
91 (1844) 5 QB 574 at 581.
92 (1844) 5 QB 574 at 582.

It was unanimously agreed that Stanley had signed the documents. Stanley had written the letters himself. He had identified himself by surname in the body of the letters. By identifying himself in this way, he had demonstrated his intention that the recipient should rely on the promise contained in the letter. The signature was, in effect, his assertion, by writing his surname within the text of the message, that the contents of the letters were to be acted upon by the recipient.[93]

A note written in the third person was accepted as a signature in the 1811 case of *Morrison v Turnour*,[94] as was an unsigned statement that began 'Mr Wilmot Parker has agreed' in an action for specific performance in respect of a contract for the purchase of a leasehold house.[95]

Deeds

In Scotland, Lord Dervaird held that a deed executed by the subscription of the granter's surname alone was not of itself improbative or invalid in the case of *American Express Europe Ltd v Royal Bank of Scotland plc*,[96] following the decision in *Gordon v Murray*[97] where it was upheld that the subscription to an assignation, being 'Fullerton of that Ilk' without a Christian name, was valid. The case of *Traquair (Earl of) v Janet Gibson*[98] in which the use of initials was considered, was also canvassed. For the modern position in Scotland, see s7(2) of the Requirements of Writing (Scotland) Act 1995.

The use of a trade name

The use of a trade name by a party may be sufficient to indicate an intention to enter into a contract, as in the case of *Johnson v Dogson*,[99] where an agent for the plaintiff signed a memorandum retained by the defendant 'for' Johnson, Johnson & Co. In *Cohen v Roche*,[100] the printed name of the firm on the front page of the auction catalogue was held to constitute a signature by Mr Roche. In reaching his judgment in this case, McCardie J considered that the insertion of the name in the catalogue served to authenticate the catalogue, and this authentication was reinforced 'in that the defendant himself wrote down in his auctioneer's book the price realized by lot 145, and also entered the names of the purchasers'.[101] However, the mere insertion of the name of the seller in a memorandum where the sale of the property was subject to the approval of the seller, even where the buyer had signed the document with his mark, did not indicate authentication of the document, and the inclusion of the name of the auctioneer on

---

93 As with the case of *Tourret v Cripps* (1879) 48 LJ Ch 567, 27 WR 706, this case was not cited in *J Pereira Fernandes SA v Mehta* [2006] EWHC 813 (Ch), [2006] 1 WLR 1543, [2006] 2 All ER 891, [2006] 1 All ER (Comm) 885, [2006] 2 Lloyd's Rep 244, [2006] 4 WLUK 182, [2006] Info TLR 203, Times, 16 May 2006, [2006] CLY 774, also known as *Metha v J Pereira Fernandes SA*.
94 (1811) 18 Ves. 175, 34 ER 1204, 18 Ves. Jun. 175, 34 ER 284.
95 *Propert v Parker* [1830] 1 Russ & M 625, 39 ER 240.
96 1989 SCLR 333, 1989 SLT 650, OH.
97 (1765) Mor. 16818.
98 (1724) Mor. 16809.
99 (1837) 6 LJ Ex 185, 1 Jur 739; 2 M & W 653, Murp & H 271, 150 ER 918.
100 [1927] 1 KB 169, [1926] 6 WLUK 88.
101 [1927] 1 KB 169 at 175–176.

the particulars of sale only acted to announce that he would sell the premises.[102] In the 1842 New York case of *Miller v Pelletier*,[103] the clerk to the auctioneer wrote down the name of the highest bidder for 7 Barclay Street, New York, in the sales book. The successful bidder subsequently took action to recover the deposit because the seller claimed they had not subscribed to the contract. The Vice-Chancellor concluded that the purchaser was bound by the addition of his name to the sales book by the clerk to the auctioneer, but in the absence of the seller's name or subscription in the sales book, the contract was void, and the deposit was returned to the buyer.

A partial signature

Sudden changes in life expectancy can cause a person, as they near the end of their life, to review the arrangements for the disposal of their worldly goods. On such occasions, ensuring the disposition is made in the proper form can be overtaken by the imminent demise of the testatrix. In *Chalcraft's Goods, Re*,[104] as Mrs Chalcraft's life ebbed away, her doctor administered greater doses of morphia to alleviate the pain she was experiencing. She wanted to sign a codicil to her will, and took hold of a pen and wrote 'E. Chal', but never completed her name because she died, and the signature came to an abrupt end. One of the issues before the court was whether what the deceased wrote was intended to be her signature. Willmer J found that whether the partial signature could be considered to be her signature within the provisions of the Wills Act 1837 was a 'very difficult point to decide'.[105] He suggested that there must be a question of degree involved in any decision, and he interpreted the words used by the Lord Chancellor in *Hindmarch v Charlton*[106] broadly. Taking into account the circumstances the deceased found herself in at the end of her life, he decided that the mark she made did amount to a signature.[107] Compare this with the case where a witness began to sign their name, but through infirmity only signed with their first name and failed to complete their name. Given such a set of facts, it was held that the witness intended to write their full name and failed to do so. This meant the signature was not a perfect subscription to the will.[108]

In comparison, in 1892 Mitchell J concluded that there was no signature where a testator began to sign a codicil, but stopped after making a stroke of the pen resembling the first part of the first letter of his name, and said to those present 'I can't sign it now'. Given the nature of the evidence, the judge concluded that the testator did not intend the scrawl on the document to be a signature.[109] The Outer House in Scotland reached the same decision in the case of *Donald v M'Gregor*,[110] where the matron of the hospital,

---

102 *Dyas v Stafford* [1882] 9 LR Ir 520.
103 4 Edw. Ch. 102 (1975).
104 [1948] P 222, [1948] 1 All ER 700, 65 TLR 246, [1948] 3 WLUK 52, [1948] LJR 1111, (1948) 92 SJ 181, [194751] CLY 10955, also known as *Chalcraft v Giles*.
105 [1948] P 222 at 232.
106 (1861) 8 HL Cas 160 at 167 'I will lay down this as my notion of the law: that to make a valid subscription of a witness, there must be the name or some mark which is intended to represent the name'.
107 In Scotland, the court held that a partial signature was not sufficient in *Moncrieff v Monypenny* [1710] Mor 15936.
108 *In the Goods of Maddock* (1874) LR 3 P & D 169.
109 *In re Plate's Estate*, 148 Pa. 55, 23 A. 1038.
110 1926 SLT 103.

at the request of the deceased, wrote a codicil on a postcard. The deceased tried to sign it, but desisted after writing 'Mary T. M'Gr', adding a cross as her mark. Two witnesses appended their signatures. Lord Ashmore noted, at 105, that 'the deceased did not herself subscribe the codicil; for although she began to write her name she did not complete it, probably because she was too weak and too ill to write more than she did, and no one executed the writing for her' and went on to indicate that in Scotland, 'as regards the cross which she added – signing by a mark is not sufficient in law'. Neither her partial signature nor the cross acted as a signature.

Words other than a name

Occasionally, people will not refer to each other by name but by reference to their relationship with each other, such as between parents and children, where a child may call their parents 'mum' and 'dad', 'mater' or 'pater', or some other form of address. Equally, parents may well do the same with their children, especially when writing to them. They may not sign a letter or card with their name, but with the words 'mother' or 'father'. In the case of *Cook, In the Estate of*,[111] the testatrix drew up a holograph will on two sheets of notepaper, which was duly properly attested by two competent witnesses. The document ended 'Please Leslie be kind to Dot. Your loving mother.' Leslie was her son and Dot referred to one of her daughters. The question was whether the words 'Your loving mother' constituted a signature within the meaning of the Wills Act 1837. Collingwood J, having cited various authorities, came to the conclusion that the testatrix intended the words 'Your loving mother' to identify herself as the person attesting.[112] This case illustrates the concern that judges have in establishing whether the person signing the document intended the words they used to apply to the terms of the document they signed.

In the United States, there is a line of case law to illustrate the use of similar words and phrases,[113] although the 1940 Californian case of *Berdan v*

---

111 [1960] 1 WLR 353, [1960] 1 All ER 689, [1960] 2 WLUK 75, 75 ALR2d 892, (1960) 104 SJ 311, [1960] CLY 3327, also known as *Murison v Cook*.
112 The most persuasive comment to support his decision in this context was the opinion of Lord Campbell LC in *Hindmarch v Charlton* (1861) 8 HL Cas 160 at 167.
113 Arkansas (1906): *Arendt v Arendt*, 80 Ark. 204, 96 S.W. 982 (after William Arendt shot himself, a letter addressed to his wife was discovered, including the statement 'Whatever I have in worldly goods, it is my wish that you should possess them'. At the end of the letter, he signed with a shortened version of his first name, 'Will'. Held to be a signature by the members of the jury and affirmed on appeal); *Boone v Boone*, 114 Ark. 69, 169 S.W. 779 (testator omitted the letter 'n' in his signature in writing his first name, Emanuel, on one of the sheets of the will; this did not affect the validity) (1914); *Cartwright v Cartwright*, 158 Ark. 278, 250 S.W. 11 (a letter sent by an American soldier killed in action on 14 October 1918 to his wife, part of which was testamentary in its effect, and signed with the abbreviation of his first name 'Lus'; held to be a sufficient signature) (1923).

California: *In re Henderson's Estate*, 196 Cal. 623, 239 P. 938 (The phrase 'From A Loving Mother' was a sufficient signature) (1923); *In re Button's Estate*, 277 P. 758 *reversed* 287 P. 964 ('Love from Muddy' was a valid signature) (1930).

Kentucky: *Word v Whipps*, 28 S.W. 151, 16 Ky. Law Rep. 403 (in the absence of fraud or suspicious circumstances, the misspelling of a name did not affect the validity of a signature: 'A. J. Whpps' written instead of 'A. J. Whipps') (1894); *Wells v Lewis*, 190 Ky. 626, 228 S.W. 3 ('Ant Nanie' appended to a letter as a testamentary writing was a sufficient signature) (1921).

Berdan[114] demonstrated that this liberal approach can only be taken so far. In this instance, a father wrote a letter to his son on a typewriter, and his wife added further handwritten script on the reverse of the letter: 'Dad signed this with his signature and also "Dad" below. The signature in case you might want to use it. Lawfully. Mother.' The word 'Mother' was capable of being a legally binding signature, but was taken not to be because it was assumed, in the absence of any evidence, that the language illustrated that she did not believe the word 'Dad' was a legally binding signature.

An identifying phrase

In contrast to the examples above, the use of the word 'mother' was not held to be a signature in an earlier case of *Selby v Selby*,[115] where a letter addressed to the son beginning 'My Dear Robert' and ending in the words 'Do me the justice to believe me the most affectionate of mothers' was not satisfactorily signed within the meaning of the Statute of Frauds 1677. The Master of the Rolls held that it was not sufficient that a party to a document can be identified in such a way because the Statute required the document to be signed. He rejected the proposition that where the writer of the document has been identified, it could therefore be construed that there was a signature within the meaning of the Statute. Lord Skerrington also concluded, in *Pentland v Pentland's Trustees*,[116] that a holograph codicil signed 'Yr Loving Mother' was not signed. The basis of the objections to accepting such terms as a form of signature were set out by Interim Sheriff-Substitute Kermack in *Allan and Crichton, Petitioners*,[117] where a witness had subscribed as 'Mrs Bernard' without adhibiting her Christian name or initial, which was not considered to form a signature.

It is instructive to compare the decision of the Master of the Rolls in *Selby v Selby* to that of the comment made by Maule J in *Morton v Copeland*, that a 'Signature does not necessarily mean writing a person's Christian and surname, but any mark which indicates it as the act of the party'.[118] This view was also considered in the case of *Sperling*,[119] where Thomas Saunders was directed by George W. Harris, solicitor to the deceased, to sign as a second witness to the will, saying 'Now sign yourself as servant to Mr. Sperling', upon which he wrote 'Servant to Mr. Sperling'. Sir J. P. Wilde held that there was sufficient attestation and subscription because he was satisfied that Mr Saunders wrote the words on the will intending to identify himself as the person attesting. The decision by Lord Hunter in *Rhodes v Peterson*[120] from Scotland reached

---

Pennsylvania (1890): *Appeal of Knox,* 131 P. 220, 18 A. 1021, 6 L.R.A. 353, 17 Am.St.Rep. 798; *In re Kimmel's Estate*, 278 P. 435, 123 A. 405, 31 A.L.R. 678 (a testamentary letter ending with 'Father' was held to be signed) (1924).

Texas: *Barnes v Horne*, 233 S.W. 859 (a letter by the deceased to his brother was considered a will, and the shortened version of his name 'Ed' at the end was accepted as a signature) (1921).

114 103 P.2d 622.
115 (1817) 3 Mer 2, 36 ER 1.
116 (1908) 16 SLT 480.
117 1933 SLT (Sh. Ct.) 2.
118 (1855) 16 CB 516 at 535. A footnote was added to this comment: 'Provided it be proved or admitted to be genuine, and be the accustomed mode of signature of the party', 139 ER 861.
119 *In the Goods of Sperling* (1863) 3 Sw. & Tr. 273, 165 ER 1279.
120 [1970] ScotCS CSOH_1, (1971) SC 56, (1972) SLT 98.

the same conclusion. In *Rhodes v Peterson*, Mrs Dorothy Macandrew wrote a letter to her daughter in her own handwriting, and signed it 'Lots of Love. Mum'. Lord Hunter was required to determine whether the word 'Mum' was sufficient to establish that the holograph will was duly signed. He noted some latitude in the law of Scotland towards the meaning of what is meant by a signature, and went on to observe, at 100(a):

> It clearly is not essential that the subscription should consist of a surname preceded by either an initial or initials or a Christian name or names, nor is it essential that the surname should appear at all or, indeed, that there should be comprised in the subscription or signature any of the Christian names or surnames written in full.

Lord Hunter also indicated that the use of a familiar or pet name could be a valid signature provided it was proved that the writer usually signed their name in such a way. He went on to suggest, at 100(b), that the use of such a form of signature was 'as apt to signify that the writing is the completed and concluded expression of the writer's intention as a signature by initials or by abbreviated Christian name'. In particular, he considered it settled authority that where a holograph writing consisted of a name other than the Christian name or names, or initials followed by the surname, of the writer, there must be sufficient evidence to identify that whatever name was used by the writer (in this case, 'Mum') was used regularly. The form by which people identify themselves does not necessarily affect the validity of the document, especially where a person writes a document with their own handwriting and uses a phrase as a means of identification.

Abbreviation of a name

Professional firms tend to accumulate long names over time, although the present fashion is to adopt a shortened version. Long names can be tedious; one partner in the firm of Bartlett Gluckstein Crawley & de Reya sought to reduce the requirement of signing the firm's name in full, and a client decided to challenge this practice.[121] Mr Byrne was sent a bill of costs. The bill had a printed heading with the full name of the partnership, its address and the names of the partners. The bill was signed 'Bartletts' by a partner. The full name was printed below the signature, but not immediately beneath it. The bill was sent with a letter headed with the firm's full name, which was also signed in the same abbreviated name. Mr Byrne refused to pay because the signature on the bill did not comply with the requirements of s69(2) of the Solicitors Act 1974. The firm brought an action to recover the costs. McDonnell J gave judgment for Mr Byrne. He accepted the sum was owed, but agreed that the bill was not signed in accordance with the required form. On appeal, Fox LJ determined that the bill was properly signed, and offered the following comments:

> There had been legislation relating to solicitors' bills of costs over several centuries. The question was whether as a matter of construction it could be said that the bill was signed 'in the name of the firm'.
>
> Those words could not require that the whole name of the firm, which in the present case was a long one, had to be set out in full. If a solicitor was required

---

121 *Bartletts de Reya v Byrne* [1983] 1WLUK 17, (1983) 133 NLJ 1101, Times, 14 January 1983, (1983) 127 SJ 69, [1983] CLY 3604.

to sign in his own name he did not have to sign all his names in full nor write all his initials.

If the name of the firm had been printed immediately below the signature 'Bartletts' it could hardly have been doubted that the bill was signed in the name of the firm.

There was a signature on the bill of costs by a solicitor of the Supreme Court. That signature was intended to authenticate the bill and the defendant treated it as a bill issued with the authority of the firm itself ....

The signature could only be regarded as a signature in the name of the firm, and anyone reading it would take it to be a convenient and obvious contraction of the full name of the firm.[122]

Bush J agreed with this analysis and the appeal was allowed. Interestingly, between the trial and the appeal a fresh bill of costs was prepared and delivered to Mr Byrne, signed with the full name of the firm. It was paid before the hearing in the Court of Appeal took place.

---

[122] Times, 14 January, 1988.

6
Marks used as signatures

A seal imprint

By way of introduction, at one time a seal may well have been considered sufficient to bind without a signature. For instance, the National Heritage Centre for Horseracing & Sporting Art in Newmarket, England, is in possession of the original indenture, dated 28 March 1654, between the Council of New Sarum and Sir Edward Bayton for the establishment of a prize fund of £320 to provide a silver-gilt cup to the value of £18 for an annual horserace on Salisbury Plain. It has been known as the City Bowl since 1813. This race was the only one that appeared in the first Historical List of 1727, and has been run ever since on a proper racecourse. The indenture is on vellum with a wax seal. There are no signatures.

Wills

The impression of a seal on documents has a long history, especially in relation to wills, and their use continues today. An early case after the passing of the Statute of Frauds where a seal was the subject of a decision is that of *Lemayne v Stanley*,[1] where the devisor wrote his will in his own hand, and added his seal to the will, but did not sign it. It was unanimously held that this was a good will because he had written it himself and identified himself in the will by name. There was disagreement as to whether the imprint of the seal was sufficient to satisfy the requirement for a signature. Three members of the court, North, Wyndham and Charlton JJ, considered signing was no more than a mark, and sealing was a sufficient mark. The report is ambiguous and states that the majority held that the mark was sufficient, because 'for *signum* is no more than a *mark*, and sealing is a sufficient *mark* that this is his *will*' (emphasis in the original). The second part of this sentence may be construed to mean either that the sealing was sufficient to authenticate that it was the devisor's will, or that the sealing was sufficient because the devisor wrote the will in his own hand and clearly identified himself.[2]

This decision may well not have been acceptable to many judges, for in *Smith v Evans*[3] Lord Chief Baron Parker and Clive and Smythe BB denounced it as 'a very strange doctrine'. It was considered that signing with a seal would open the possibilities of forgery, a comment that reflected a change in judicial attitude from the Middle Ages, indicating the reduced importance given to a seal in England and Wales. In a later case, that of *Warneford v Warneford*,[4] Raymond CJ ruled that the sealing of a will was also a

---

1   (1681) 3 Lev 2, 83 ER 545.
2   In the case of *Dormer v Thurland* (1728) 2 Eq Ca Abr 663, 22 ER 557, 2 P Wms 506, 24 ER 837, a will had to be signed and sealed to be effective, and because it was signed but not sealed, it was declared void for want of being sealed.
3   (1751) 1 Wils K B 313, 95 ER 636.
4   (1727) (Easter 13 Geo 1) 2 Strange 764, 93 ER 834.

signing within the Statute of Frauds 1677. The report of this case is merely a statement of the decision, which does not make it a persuasive authority. In any event, this case predated the comments made in *Smith v Evans*. The reporting of decisions such as this were clearly in the mind of a later Chief Justice when he commented upon this issue in *Ellis v Smith*.[5] Willes CJ quashed the notion that a seal could be a substitute for a signature:

> Nor do I think, sealing is to be considered as signing; and I declare so now, because, if that question ever comes before me, I shall not think myself precluded from weighing it thoroughly and decreeing, that it is not signing, notwithstanding *obiter dicta*, which in many cases were *nunquam dicta*; but barely the words of reporters; for upon examination I have found many of the sayings ascribed to that great man, Lord Chief Justice *Holt*, were never said by him.[6]

Two arguments were put forward to distrust a seal. In *Grayson v Atkinson*,[7] the Lord Chancellor suggested that it was not possible to determine whose seal was used:

> how can it be said, that putting a seal to it would be a sufficient signing? For any one may put a seal; no particular evidence arises from that seal: common seals are alike, and one man's may be like another's; no certainty or guard therefore arises from thence.[8]

Another reason for rejecting the use of a seal was given by Sir John Strange,[9] suggesting that the nature of a seal was such that it cannot serve to identify an act:

> that sealing is signing, I am not convinced; for sealing identifies nothing; it carries no character ... and most seals are affixed by the stationers, who prepare the paper.

It seems the court in the case of *Ellis v Smith* had sufficient weight of authority, comprising, as it did, the Lord Chancellor, Master of the Rolls, Chief Justice and Chief Baron, to prevent future submissions that a seal could be a substitute for a signature.

A further variation of the use of a seal occurred in the case of *Re Emerson's Goods*,[10] where a handwritten document ended with the words 'Signed, sealed, and delivered by me, the first day of February, 1881'. The seal marked, with his initials, was added in the presence of the subscribing witnesses, and the testator also placed one of his fingers on the wax impression and stated before the witnesses 'This is my last will, and this is my hand and seal'. Warren J granted probate on the basis that the testator used the words 'this is my hand', intending this statement to be his signature. This decision was followed by Warren J in the case of *R Lemon's Goods*,[11] where the testator was too ill to write, so he stamped his initials in wax on the paper in the presence of the witnesses.

Interest in real property

Seals used to be attached to an indenture respecting an interest in property, and Lord Eldon LC took up the discussion relating to the use of a seal in the case of *Wright*

---

5 (1754) 1 Ves Jun 11; 1 Ves Jun Supp 1; 30 ER 205, 34 ER 666.
6 (1754) 1 Ves Jun 11 at 13 [emphasis in original].
7 (1752) 2 Ves Sen 455, 28 ER 291; Ves Sen Supp 382, 28 ER 556.
8 28 ER 556 at 292.
9 *Ellis v Smith* (1754) 1 Ves Jun 11 at 13 and 15.
10 (1882–23) 9 LR Ir Ch 443.
11 (1896) 30 IrLTR 127.

v Wakeford,[12] where indentures were signed, sealed and delivered. However, the memorandum of attestation stated only that they were signed and delivered. Bearing in mind the value of the estate, at £15,988, this became a technical issue of great importance to both parties. After the death of Thomas Wood the elder, who was a party to the indenture, the two attesting witnesses endorsed a further memorandum, stating they witnessed the signing at the same time as the original document was sealed and delivered. Eldon LC rejected the proposition that a subsequent attestation was acceptable. He accepted that the document may have been signed, sealed and delivered, but it was not attested to this effect. As a consequence, he held that the members of a jury could not presume that the act of signing was done in the presence of the attesting witnesses. In comparison to the other cases cited in relation to whether a seal is sufficient as a signature, the decision in this case was decided upon the technical issue of regularity of the attestation. Lord Eldon took the opportunity, at 458–459, to make further observations about the use of a seal as a means of authentication:

> It is true, at one time it was decided, that sealing was signing (*Lemayne v Stanly*, 3 *Lev.* 1. *Warneford v Warneford*, 2 *Sir.* 764); and when it was urged, that the Legislature meant more than sealing, first, from the circumstance, that sealing is not mentioned as to Wills: secondly, as the Legislature must have proposed some evidence from the hand-writing of the party, the objection was, that a person may sign by his mark: an act affording no material testimony; and upon such reasoning it was decided originally, that sealing was signing: but upon a review of that the contrary has been held for a long time; and, so far as sealing from being equivalent to signing, that it is determined, that sealing is not necessarily; and that sealing without signing is not a sufficient execution of a Will (see *Ellis v Smith*, 1 *Ves, jun.* 11; and that attestation by a mark is good, *Harrison v Harrison, Addy v Grix*, 8 *Ves.* 185, 405): the converse holding as to a deed; which cannot be without sealing and delivery: if signed, it may be a writing: but, if delivered, it may be a good deed, whether signed, or not, and, if it is to be executed under a power with signature and sealing, both are required.

This decision may have been unique to the facts of the case given the value of the estate in question, and can be distinguished from *Re Emerson's Goods*[13] for this reason.

By comparison, another technicality arose in *Lord Lovelace's Case*,[14] where a swaynemoote roll was authenticated with one seal by an officer of the forest by the assent of all the verders, regarders and other officers.[15] In this instance, it

---

12 (1811) 17 Ves Jun 455, 34 ER 176.
13 (1882–83) 9 LR Ir Ch 443.
14 (c1632) W Jones, 268, 82 ER 140, W Jones, 270, 82 ER 141.
15 The words 'swaynemoote' and 'verder' do not appear in the Oxford English Dictionary (2nd edn on CDROM, version 4.0, 2009). A regarder is defined as 'an officer charged with the supervision of a forest'. Some references in the OED in relation to this definition include the following:

1594 CROMPTON *Jurisd.* 169 If a man be indited of Trespasse done in the forrest before verdors, regardors, agistors, and other Ministers of the Forrest [etc.].

1667-8 *Act 19 & 20 Chas. II*, c. 8 s5 New Elections shall be made ... of all Verderors, Reguarders and other Officers of and for the Governing of the said Forrest [of Dean].

1865 *Morn. Star 13 Apr.*, The Crown have neglected to appoint a warden, forester, regarder, and verderer of the said [Epping] forest.

was held that a single seal was a good obligation of them all. Similarly, in *Ball v Dunsterville*[16] one partner executed a deed for himself and his partner, by authority of the partner and in his presence. This act was a sufficient execution, even though only one seal was used. In *Cooch v Goodman*,[17] two people entered into a lease in their capacity as governors of a hospital. The defendant signed the lease and added his seal, and the lessors affixed a common seal to the lease, but did not sign it. No decision was made, because the seal was that of a corporation, not of the individuals, which meant the wrong parties initiated the action. Lord Denman CJ commented, at 598, that a single seal might serve a number of people:

> It is true that one piece of wax may serve as a seal for several persons, if each of them impress it himself, or one for all, by proper authority, or in the presence of all, as was held in *Ball v Dunsterville* (4 T.R. 313), following *Lord Lovelace's Case* (W. Jones, 268).

More recently, the case of *First National Securities Ltd v Jones*[18] considered the effect on a legal charge sealed with a circle printed on the document containing the letters 'L.S.' with the signature of the first defendant affixed across the seal. It was held to be sufficiently executed where the seal had been placed with the intention of serving the purpose of a seal. Buckely LJ indicated at 118 C–D:

> it is a very familiar feature nowadays of documents which are intended to be executed as deeds that they do not have any wax, or even wafer, seal attached to them, but have printed at the spot where formerly the seal would probably have been placed, a printed circle, which is sometimes hatched and sometimes the letters 'L.S.' within it, which is intended to serve the purpose of a seal if the document is delivered as the deed of the party executing it.

> In the present case there is not only the circle with the letters 'L.S.' within it upon the document, printed as part of the printed version of the document, but also there is the feature that the mortgagor has placed his signature across the circle. In my judgment those features and the attestation, in the absence of any contrary evidence, are sufficient evidence to establish that the document was executed by the first defendant as his deed.

Goff LJ emphasized at 119 E that the intent behind the act was important: 'In my judgment, in this day and age, we can, and we ought to, hold that a document purporting to be a deed is capable in law of being such although it has no more than an indication where the seal should be', and Sir David Cairns suggested at 121 B what the modern view might be on the use of seals: 'Moreover, while in 1888 the printed indication of a *locus sigilli* was regarded as being merely the place where a seal was to be affixed, I have no doubt that it is now regarded by most business people and ordinary members of the public as constituting the seal itself.' The decision reached in this more recent case mirrors the approach taken by the members of the court in

---

See Jean Birrell, 'Common rights in the medieval forest: disputes and conflicts in the thirteenth century', (1987) 117 Past & Present 22, where the author indicates, at 24, 'Unfortunately, evidence about common rights in the medieval period is surprisingly difficult to find'. A swaynemoote roll might have been a document setting out rights before a manorial, royal or forest court (Birrell, 25).

16 (1791) 4 TR 313, 100 ER 1038.
17 (1842) 2 QB 580, 114 ER 228.
18 [1978] Ch 109, [1978] 2 WLR 475, [1978] 2 All ER 221, [1977] 11 WLUK 24, (1977) 121 SJ 760, Times, 9 November 1977, [1978] CLY 793.

Re Sandilands,[19] where a deed had pieces of green ribbon attached to places where the seals should be, but no wax or other material to receive an impression. It was held there was sufficient evidence that the deed was sealed. Bovill CJ observed, at 413, 'Here is something attached to this deed which may have been intended for a seal, but which from its nature is incapable of retaining an impression', while Byles J also offered the opinion at 413 that 'The sealing of a deed need not be by means of a seal; it may be done with the end of a ruler or anything else'.

Court records

Despite the reluctance of some judges to accept a seal as a signature in the eighteenth century, the members of the Exchequer of Pleas in the nineteenth century decided a seal was sufficient in relation to office copies from the Insolvent Court, being a court of record, in the case of *Doe d. Phillips, Jones, and Morris v Evans and Lloyd*.[20] It was possible for an office copy to be adduced as evidence without further proof, although it had to be signed by an officer of the court. Having discussed the relevant statutory provisions in his judgment, Bayley B came to the conclusion that where an office copy was sealed with the seal of the Insolvent Debtors' Court, 'The seal of the Court then becomes the signature of the Court and of the officer'.[21] It seems that this decision provided for the authentication of the insolvency petition either where the document contained the signature of the officer or his deputy and the seal of the court, or where the document only contained the seal of the court. Given the comment by Bayley B, it appears that the seal of the court was sufficient for the purpose of authentication. In *R v St Paul, Covent Garden Inhabitants*,[22] relating to the settlement of an illegitimate child, it was not considered necessary that an order of the justices be sealed with wax. Two Justices of the Peace signed the order. The order was made on a pre-printed form. From time to time the parish officers of St Martin in the Fields caused a printer to print a large number of the forms, and on each sheet a stationer was employed to impress two marks in ink with wooden blocks, and these impressions, when made at the foot, were intended to serve as seals for the justices when they signed such orders. The court in the Quarter Sessions held that the impression in ink made by such blocks was a sufficient seal to make the order, and when signed and delivered by the justices, it constituted a good and valid order.

In the United States, seals have generally been upheld, although there seems to have been a divergence between adopting the word 'seal' as an acknowledgement that a document has been sealed, and refusing to accept a document has been sealed unless an impression of a seal has been affixed.[23] Recognition of the Japanese seal is illustrated in the Pennsylvanian case of *Zenith Radio Corporation v Matsushita Electric Industrial Co., Ltd*,[24] where Becker DJ commented, at 1224, that a Japanese seal 'should be given weight equivalent to a signature'. The 1916 New York case of

---

19 (1871) LR 6 CP 411.
20 (1833) 1 C & M 450, 149 ER 476, (1833) LJ Ex 2 NS 179.
21 (1833) 1 C & M 450 at 461.
22 (1844) 5 QB 671, 114 ER 1402, (1845) 7 QB 232, 115 ER 476.
23 For a list of cases relating to the adoption of seals, see Richard A. Lord, *Williston on Contracts* (4th edn, Thompson West 1990), 2:2.
24 505 F.Supp. 1190 (1980).

Matter of the Probate of the Will of Severance[25] dealt with an unusual form of seal. The testator affixed a holiday seal (containing the inscription 'Merry Christmas. American Red Cross, 1912 Happy New Year') to his will and inscribed it with his initials. It was held to constitute a subscription where the testator intended the holiday seal and inscription as a signature.

The use of a fingerprint

In the same way that a mark is accepted as a form of signature, in what seems to be a unique case in England the impression of a thumb smeared in ink was accepted as a signature, although Langton J commented that the method did not commend itself to him.[26] Thumb prints are also accepted in South Africa,[27] and in China where, if a party affixes a fingerprint to a contract, it has the same effect as a signature or stamp.[28]

The use of a printed name

Statute of Frauds

The legal constraints relating to commerce were gradually amended during the nineteenth century, and the case of *Saunderson v Jackson*[29] at the beginning of that century serves to illustrate how the judges began to deal with the practical issues relating to contractual disputes where the 'signature' was affixed by the use of technology. In this instance, a bill of parcels was delivered, part of which was printed with 'London. Bought of Jackson and Hankin, distillers, No 8 Oxford Street' and there followed in manuscript writing '1000 gallons of gin, 1 in 5 gin £350 7s'. A dispute occurred, and Lord Eldon articulated the single question as follows: 'Whether if a man be in the habit of printing instead of writing his name, he may not be said to sign by his printed name as well as his written name?'[30] In this instance, the bill of parcels was not considered to be of sufficient evidence on its own to be viewed as a note or memorandum of the contract, although a subsequent letter signed by one of the parties acted to connect the two documents, and thus took the matter outside the Statute of Frauds.

---

25   96 Misc. 384, 161 N.Y.S. 452.
26   *Re Finn* (1935) 105 LJP 36; both parties accepted that a thumb print was capable of being a signature in the case of *Borman v Lel* [2001] 6 WLUK 189, [2002] WTLR 237, [2002] CLY 4329 also known as: *Parsons, In the Estate of*. Although use of fingerprints as a signature was probably common in some parts of the world at one time, for which see Iris Agmon, 'Recording procedures and legal culture in the late Ottoman Shariʻa court of Jaffa, 1865–1890' (2004) 11(3) Islamic Law and Society 333, 333377, 360361; as a result of the changes described by Agmon, the signatures of women began to be recorded for the first time, indicating the possibility that women initiated or took part in legal proceedings, 363–364.
27   *Putter v Provincial Insurance Co. Ltd*, 1963 (3) SA 145 (W).
28   'Supreme People's Court, interpretation on several issues concerning the application of the PRC contract law' (2009) 23 China Law & Practice 41, 69.
29   (1800) 2 Bos & Pul 238, 126 ER 1257.
30   (1800) 2 Bos & Pul 238 at 239.

The later case of *Schneider v Norris*[31] distinguished the facts in *Saunderson v Jackson*.[32] In this instance, Messrs John Schneider bought cotton yarn and piece goods from Thomas Norris, who acted as agents. The bill of parcels read as follows: 'London, 24 October 1812. Messrs John Schneider and Co bought of Thomas Norris and Co, Agents. Cotton yarn and piece goods. No 3 Freeman's Court, Cornhill', all of which was printed, except the words 'Messrs John Schneider and Co', which were handwritten by an agent or employee of the defendant. The defendant refused to deliver the yarn. At the subsequent trial, the defendants did not accept that a contract had been formed, and relied on the absence of a note or memorandum in writing of the contract, as required by the Statute of Frauds 1677. Lord Ellenborough CJ overruled this objection and Schneider and Co obtained a verdict. On appeal, Lord Ellenborough reiterated his opinion at the trial, and considered that the printed name of the defendants, as it appeared on the bill, was recognized as a signature. This occurred when the name 'Messrs John Schneider and Co' was added to the bill of parcels that included the printed name of Norris and Co. By writing the name of the firm on the bill, Schneiders identified themselves with the other party to the transaction. Le Blanc and Bayley JJ concurred with this decision, and Dampier J added that the act of a person handwriting the name of the plaintiffs on the bill served to authenticate it as a memorandum of the bargain struck between the parties, and went on to explain, at 290: 'The defendant has ratified the sale to Schneider and Co by inserting their name as buyer to a paper in which he recognizes himself as seller'. Thus the names of the two firms on the same bill provided evidence of the agreement.

There is a fine distinction between these two cases. The additional manuscript comments to the bill of parcels in *Saunderson v Jackson* referred to the price and quantity of the order. This was not considered sufficient evidence, in the absence of the later signed letter, to demonstrate that a contract existed. In comparison, the additional manuscript comments in the bill of parcels in *Schneider v Norris* contained the name of one of the parties to the contract. This meant that both parties to the contract in *Schneider v Norris* were identified in the bill of parcels, and this was sufficient to establish a commercial relationship between them.[33]

At the same time as these cases were being determined, another problem of a similar nature occurred in circumstances where one of the parties retained evidence of the orders they received in loose cases and memorandum books. The 1809 case of *Allen v Bennet*[34] illustrated the problem. Wright, the agent for Bennett, agreed to sell goods to Allen, writing the orders into a book owned by Allen. The book was described as 'a sort of waste book, containing various memoranda of different natures'. Mr Allen's name was not written upon or in any part of the book. Bennett failed to deliver the

31 (1814) 2 M & S 237, 105 ER 388.
32 (1800) 2 Bos & Pul 238, 126 ER 1257.
33 In *Hubert v Treherne* (1842) 3 Man & G 743, 133 ER 1338 the names of the parties appeared in the body of a draft agreement that neither party had signed: it was held that the agreement was not signed. Both *Saunderson v Jackson* and *Schneider v Norris* were cited, and Tindal CJ indicated, at 754, that the decision in *Saunderson v Jackson* depended 'for its authority more upon the subsequent recognition than upon the printed names'.
34 (1809) 3 Taunt. 169, 128 ER 67; the spelling of Bennet differs as between the name of the case and the description of the firm in the report.

goods. It was considered that the orders entered by the agent for Bennett were made in that capacity, and in conjunction with the exchange of correspondence between the parties, this was sufficient as a memorandum and a signature by Bennett. Mansfield CJ observed a wider question that occupied the courts on this issue at the time when he said, at 176:

> every one knows it is the daily practice of the Court of Chancery to establish contracts signed by one person only, and yet a court of equity can no more dispense with the statute of frauds than a court of law can, there is no reason therefore to set aside the verdict, and the rule must be discharged.

A similar set of facts occurred in 1856 in the case of *Sarl v Bourdillon*,[35] where the defendant, about to go to India, ordered goods from the plaintiff. Having selected the goods, a list of them was entered into an order book retained for the purpose, with the words 'Order Book' printed in gold letters on the outside and the names 'Sarl & Son' written on the flyleaf at the beginning. At the foot of the entry, the plaintiff wrote the name and address of the defendant. The defendant failed to pay for the goods, and claimed there was no sufficient memorandum of the sale as required by s17 of the Statute of Frauds. It was held that the names of the contracting parties sufficiently appeared to satisfy the statute.[36] The judgments did not explain the reasoning for this decision. Jervis CJ indicated at the end of the submissions by counsel that there was only one point worth considering at length, and merely commented, at 195, that 'We also think that the names of the contracting parties sufficiently appear, to satisfy the statute of frauds'. Cresswell J delivered the judgment of the court more fully at a later date, and he said, at 195:

> In this case, inasmuch as the defendant declined to go to the jury, and insisted that there was no evidence of a memorandum to satisfy the statute of frauds, it may be assumed that the defendant wrote his name in the plaintiff's book, intending it as a signature to an order to the plaintiffs, whose order-book it was, and whose names were written in the beginning of it in the usual way. This, with the observations made in the course of argument, disposes of all the objections raised.

It is interesting to note that Cresswell J mentioned that the name 'Sarl & Son' was written in the front of the order book 'in the usual way'. It might be inferred from this comment that Cresswell J was referring to the usual method of taking an order, and that it was common knowledge that notebooks containing pages to enter orders were widely used. If this was the case, the importance of this decision should not go unnoticed, because a decision the other way would have caused business people to alter the way they conducted business, and it is usually the case that judges in England and Wales looked to the common custom in reaching a decision.[37]

---

35 (1856) 1 CB (NS) 188, 140 ER 79.
36 *Jacob v Kirk* (1839) 2 M & R 221, 174 ER 269 was argued on different facts.
37 In *Joshua Buckton and Co. (Limited) v London and North-Western Railway Company* (1917–18) 34 TLR 119 a contract signed with the printed name of the firm 'Joshua Buckton and Co. (Limited)' was accepted by Astbury J as a regular business practice at 121: 'having regard to the long practice of signing these consignment notes and to the fact that notes so signed have been accepted and recognized by the Court as fulfilling the requirements of the section', the printed name was a signature under the provisions of s7 of the Railway and Canal Traffic Act 1854.

The use of a printed name was also challenged in the case of *Evans v Hoare*[38] where an employer authorized a clerk to draw up a contract of employment, which was signed by the employee, as follows:

> 5, Campbell-terrace, Cannhill Road, Leytonstone, E. Feb 19, 1890. Messrs Hoare, Marr, and Co., 26, 29, Budge Row, London, EC. Gentlemen, In consideration of your advancing my salary to the sum of £130 per annum, I hereby agree to continue my engagement in your office for three years, from and commencing January 1, 1890, at a salary at the rate of £130 per annum as aforesaid, payable monthly as hitherto. Yours obediently, George E Evans.

The members of the jury found a verdict for Mr Evans, but the assistant judge of the Mayor's Court did not accept there was a memorandum signed by the firm in accordance with s4 of the Statute of Frauds 1677, so gave judgment for the defendants. This decision was reversed on appeal on the basis that the clerk was authorized by the firm to draw up the document.[39] Reference was made to the firm by the use of 'your' in the text and the name of the firm was included at the top of the document. The comments by Cave J reflected the difference in procedure between the passing of the statute and the time this case was heard:

> The Statute of Frauds was passed at a period when the legislature was somewhat inclined to provide that cases should be decided according to fixed rules, rather than to leave it to the jury to consider the effect of the evidence in each case. This, no doubt, arose to a certain extent from the fact that in those days the plaintiff and the defendant were not competent witnesses ... No doubt, in attempting to frame a principle, one is obliged to depart somewhat from the strict lines of the statutes.[40]

A variation of this theme, which also indicated the way people conducted their daily business, is illustrated by the case of *Jones Brothers v Joyner*,[41] where an order for hops was written down in a notebook owned by the Jones Brothers, and Joyner signed the order. The paper book in which this order was placed was, in turn, slipped into a leather cover, upon which the name 'James Jones' was stamped. When the paper memorandum book was full, it could be withdrawn and a fresh one inserted in the same leather cover. Mr Joyner contended there was no sufficient memorandum to satisfy s4 of the Statute of Frauds, as re-enacted by s4 of the Sale of Goods Act 1893, because the name of the plaintiff did not appear in the memorandum signed by him. Jones Brothers contended that the name on the cover constituted a sufficient signing. Sir Richard Harington held that the cover and the book were two distinct articles, distinguishing the decision in the case of *Sarl v Bourdillon*. The decision at first instance was reversed on appeal before Darling and Bucknell JJ. In reaching his decision, Darling J focused on the relationship between the notebook and the cover, at 769:

---

38 [1892] 1 QB 593, (1892) 66 LTR NS 345.
39 A hop factor is capable of acting as the agent for both parties to a contract: *Durrell v Evans* (1862) 1 H & C 174, 31 LJ Ex 337, 9 Jur NS 104, 10 WR 665, 7 LT 97, 158 ER 848, Ex Ch; an auctioneer was an authorized agent for the vendor where the auctioneer entered the name of the vendor on a printed agreement form for the sale of real property: *Leeman v Stocks* [1951] 1 Ch 941, [1951] 1 All ER 1043, [1951] 2 TLR 622, [1951] 4 WLUK 30, (1951) 95 SJ 368, [1947–51] CLY 10616.
40 [1892] 1 QB 593 at 597. For a more robust and less polished version of this part of the decision by Cave J, see (1892) 66 LTRep NS 345 at 347.
41 (1900) 82 LTNS 768.

when the memorandum was made they were only one. Take the case of the letter and envelope. First of all the letter is written, it is placed in an envelope, and the name of the other person appears on the envelope. In such a case there may be two distinct articles, which are used as one. Further, I think it makes no difference that the words 'order book' do not appear. In fact, the orders were placed in a book which was used for that purpose.[42]

Real property

Hall VC in *Tourret v Cripps*,[43] where Mr Cripps wrote in his own hand on a sheet of memorandum paper an offer to lease property, followed the principles set out in *Schneider v Norris*.[44] The memorandum was not signed, but contained, at its head, the words 'From Richd. L Cripps' and his address. Tourret accepted the offer, and was subsequently granted judgment for specific performance. The letter was in the handwriting of Cripps, it contained his name and it was actually sent by him, thus the court inferred that his intention was to grant the lease, and his name at the head of the letter authenticated this intention.[45] In Ireland, the members of the Supreme Court reached a similar conclusion in the case of *Casey v Irish Intercontinental Bank Limited*,[46] where a memorandum for the sale of a property was typed on the headed notepaper of the auctioneers, with the names of the directors printed at the bottom of the letter. The only manuscript signature was that of the buyer.

Public notices

The use of a printed name was beginning to be used by local authorities in the late nineteenth century. In the case of *Brydges (Town Clerk of Cheltenham) v Dix*,[47] the Cheltenham council required the town clerk to execute certain works. When the owner of the property refused, the council sent a notice to the owner on a printed form, duly filled in, with the name of the town clerk printed at the foot of the notice. The council subsequently undertook the work and then sought to recover their costs. Matters dealing with the authenticity of the notice were set out in s266 of the Public Health Act 1875, as follows:

> Notices, orders, and other such documents under the Act may be in writing or print, or partly in writing and partly in print, and if the same require authentication by the local authority the signature thereof by the clerk to the local authority, or their surveyor or inspector, shall be sufficient authentication.

---

42 Compare the decisions in *Champion v Plummer* (1805) 5 Esp. 239, 170 ER 798, 1 Bos. & P. (NR) 252, 127 ER 458; *Allen v Bennet* (1810) 3 Taunt. 169, 128 ER 67; *Jacob v Kirk* (1839) 2 M & R 221, 174 ER 269.
43 (1879) 48 L J Ch 567, 27 WR 706; these cases were reviewed by Buckley J in *Hucklesby v Hook* (1900) 82 LT 117.
44 (1814) 2 M & S 237, 105 ER 388.
45 As with the case of *Lobb and Knight v Stanley* (1844) 5 QB 574, 114 ER 1366; (1843–44) Law Times, 2, 366, this case was not cited in *J Pereira Fernandes SA v Mehta* [2006] EWHC 813 (Ch), [2006] 1 WLR 1543, [2006] 2 All ER 891, [2006] 1 All ER (Comm) 885, [2006] 2 Lloyd's Rep 244, [2006] 4 WLUK 182, [2006] Info TLR 203, Times, 16 May 2006, [2006] CLY 774.
46 [1979] IR 364.
47 (1890–91) 7 TLR 215.

An objection was made that the signature of the clerk was a requisite and that it should be affixed by hand. The magistrates accepted this argument and refused to make an order for payment. Pollock B and Charles J heard the appeal in the Queen's Bench Division. They allowed the appeal and came to the conclusion that if a signature was required, a manual signature was not necessary: 'all that was necessary was that the notice should be authenticated as coming from the town clerk, and that sufficiently appeared in this notice.'[48] The printed signature was held to be sufficient. This observation was also to be noted by Romer LJ in *Goodman v J Eban Limited*,[49] where he pointed out that the recipient could verify the authenticity of the notice by confirming its contents directly with the clerk.

Generally, judges in the United States, in combination with the approach adopted in various model acts to provide a degree of uniformity to the law, have agreed with their brethren in England. The range of illustrations includes printing on bank notes,[50] bills of lading,[51] bonds,[52] brokers contracts[53] and court papers[54] – although printed names have

---

48 (1890–91) 7 TLR 215 at 216(a).
49 [1954] 1 QB 550 at 564.
50 Federal, 7th circuit: *Hill v United States*, 288 F. 192 (the facsimile signatures of the governor and cashier of the Federal Reserve Bank of St Louis on bank notes were true and genuine signatures) (1923).
51 Pennsylvania: *Carna t/d/b/a/ T.C. Trucking Company v Bessemer Cement Company*, 558 F.Supp. 706 (1983) (the pre-printed company name on a bill of lading was held to be a sufficient signature).
52 California: *Pennington v Baehr*, 48 Cal. 565, 1874 WL 1399 (Cal.) (a bond signed by a printed facsimile of the signature of the president of the Reclamation Fund Commissioners was held to be sufficient) (1874). It is reported that the Attorney-General argued, at 567, that 'A printed *fac simile* ... could be more easily forged than an autograph; and such a signature would be no more protection than no signing at all'; *Williams v McDonald*, 58 Cal. 527, 8 P.C.L.J. 23, 58 Cal. 527, 1881 WL 1946 (Cal.) (a resolution of intention with the printed name of the clerk affixed was sufficient because he intended the printed name to be adopted).
53 Nebraska: *Berryman v Childs*, 98 Neb. 450, 153 N.W. 486 (where the plaintiffs signed a contract with their printed name, they were entitled to the benefit of that contract) (1915).
54 California: *Hancock v Bowman*, 49 Cal. 413, 1874 WL 1548 (Cal.) (a judgment was not void because the name of the plaintiff's attorney is printed on the complaint) (1874); *Ligare v California Southern Railroad Company*, 76 Cal. 610, 18 P. 777 (a summons signed with the printed signature of the clerk accompanied with the seal of the court was held to be sufficient signature) (1888); *Smith v Ostly*, 53 Cal.2d 262, 1 Cal.Rptr. 340, 347 P.2d 684 (a name printed on a notice of appeal could be adopted as a signature providing the petitioner intended to authenticate the document) (1959).

Indiana: *Hamilton v State*, 103 Ind. 96, 2 N.E. 299, 53 AmRep. 491 (it was sufficient that the name of the prosecuting attorney appeared in print on an indictment) (1885).

Iowa (1908): *Cummings v Landes*, 117 N.W. 22, 140 Iowa 80 (an original notice was signed when the name of the attorney was printed thereon).

Minnesota: *Ames v Schurmeier*, 9 Minn. 221, 1864 WL 1409 (Minn.), 9 Gil. 206 (a summons in a civil action was void where the name of the plaintiff or their attorney was printed where handwriting was required); *Herrick v Morrill*, 37 Minn. 250, 33 N.W. 849, 5 Am.St.Rep. 841 (a summons in a civil action may be subscribed by the printed signature of the plaintiff or his attorney) (1887).

New York: *Barnard v Heydrick*, 49 Barb. 62, 32 How. Pr. 97, 2 Abb.Pr.N.S. 47 (a summons issued by an attorney with his name typed at the end was subscribed by him within the meaning of the provisions of the Code of Procedure) (1866). Note the cases cited and discussion of the decision of Ingraham J in *The Farmers' Loan and Trust Company v Dickson*, 9 Abb.Pr. 61 (1859).

Wisconsin: *Mezchen v More*, 54 Wis. 214, 11 N.W. 534 (a summons in a civil action with the printed names of the attorneys was subscribed) (1882).

not always been accepted[55] and a printed name can be the subject of forgery (including a name on a rubber stamp)[56] – promissory notes (subject to suitable evidence),[57] public documents,[58] Statute of Frauds generally (with rare exceptions),[59] with respect

---

55 Arkansas: *Lee v Vaughan Seed Store*, 101 Ark 68 (1911), 141 S.W. 496, 37 L.R.A.N.S. 352 (a printed name was not accepted as evidence of authentication); California: *Marks v Walter G. McCarty Corporation*, 33 Cal.2d 814 (1949), 205 P.2d 1025; New York: *The Farmers' Loan and Trust Company v Dickson*, 9 Abb. Pr. 61 (a summons issued by an attorney with his name typed at the end was a nullity) (1859).
56 Massachusetts: *Commonwealth v Ray*, 3 Gray 441, 69 Mass. 441, 1855 WL 5701 (Mass.) (a printed or engraved name can be forged) (1855); *Wellington v Jackson*, 121 Mass. 157, 1876 WL 10902 (Mass.) (a person who knows a signature is forged on a promissory note, but who acknowledges it as his own, assumes the note to be his as if it was signed with his authority).
Oklahoma: *Boyer v State*, 68 Okl.Cr. 220, 97 P. 779 (a person can forge a name if they use a rubber stamp) (1939).
57 Illinois: *Weston v Myers*, 33 Ill. 424, 1864 WL 2948 (Ill.) (a printed name adopted on an instrument for value).
Minnesota: *Brayley v Kelly*, 25 Minn. 160, 1878 WL 3577 (Minn) (a printed name on a promissory note was not admissible as the act of the party without further evidence).
Oregon: *Toon v Wapinitia Irrigation Co.*, 117 Or. 374, 243 P. 554 (a printed signature attached to an interest coupon payable to the bearer was sufficient to authenticate the instrument) (1926).
58 North Carolina: *State of North Carolina v Watts*, 289 N.C. 445, 222 S.E.2d 389 (the mechanical reproduction of the name of an authorized officer placed on a public record was properly authenticated where the officer intended to adopt the mechanical reproduction as his signature) (1976).
Wisconsin: *Potts v Cooley*, 13 N.W.Rep. 682 (a tax certificate with the words 'Assigned May 19, 1877. J P. Carpenter, County Clerk' partly written by hand and partly printed on the face of the certificate was sufficient for the purposes of the statue) (1882).
59 Arizona: *Bishop v Norelld/b/a Al Norell Company Realtors*, 88 Ariz. 148, 353 P.2d 1022 (a name and address printed on a listing agreement was signed in accordance with the statute provided it was done with the intention of signing) (1960).
Georgia: *Kohlmeyer & Company v Bowen*, 126 Ga.App. 700, 192 S.E.2d 400 (the name of a securities brokerage firm printed on a confirmation statement for the sale of securities was held to be intended as a means of authentication and thus met the signature requirement under the Statute of Frauds) (1972). Note the dissenting judgment of Evans J and his comments in respect of *Evans Implement Company v Thomas Industries, Inc.*, 117 Ga.App. 279, 160 S.E.2d 462, (Ga. Ct. App. 1968).
Idaho: *Paloukos v Intermountain Chevrolet Company*, 99 Idaho 740 (1978), 588 P.2d 939, 25 UCC Rep. Serv. 655.
Illinois: *Prairie State Grain and Elevator Company v Wrede*, 217 Ill.App. 407 (the name 'Ben. B. Bishopp, Grain Broker' printed on a memorandum was sufficient for it to have been adopted and signed by him as if this text had been personally placed on the memorandum, especially because he had used such a signature for years) (1920).
Kansas: *Southwest Engineering Company, Inc. v Martin Tractor Company, Inc.*, 205 Kan. 684, 473 P.2d 18 (the name 'Ken Hurt, Martin Tractor, Topeka, Caterpillar' printed on a memorandum with the details of specifications for a generator written by hand was sufficient authentication) (1970).
Michigan: *Grieb v Cole*, 60 Mich. 397, 27 N.W. 579, 1 Am.St.Rep. 533 (a warranty printed on the back of a purchase order with the vendor's printed signature binds the warrantor) (1886).
Missouri: *Defur v Westinghouse Electric Corporation*, 677 F.Supp. 622 (E.D.Mo. 1988) (a Relocation Policy/Home Sale Program had the defendant's name printed on every page, and was held to constitute a writing signed by the defendant).
New York: *Vielie v Osgood*, 8 Barb. 130 (names printed at the foot of a contract were held not to be a sufficient subscription within the Statute of Frauds) (1849); 1913 case of *Goldowitz v Henry Kupfer & Co.*, 80 Misc.Rep. 487, 141 N.Y.S. 531; 1920 cases of *Pearlberg v Levisohn*, 112 Misc. 95, 182 N.Y.S. 615 and *United Display Fixture Co., Inc. v S. & W. Bauman*, 183 N.Y.S. 4.; *Cohen v Arthur Walker & Co., Inc.*, 192 N.Y.S. 228 (the printed name of the defendant corporation on an order for goods was sufficient compliance

to letterheads[60] and in matters pertaining to voting.[61] The burden of proving a printed name was adopted is on the party asserting the nature of the signature, as illustrated by the 1949 Californian case of *Felt v L. B. Frederick Co., Inc.*[62] In addition, care must be taken over proving the link between the printed name or letterhead and the intent to authenticate, as in the 1949 Californian case of *Marks v Walter G. McCarty Corporation*,[63] where use of letterhead stationery containing the name of a hotel to provide carbon copies was not sufficient to show intention to adopt the letterhead as a signature, as indicated by Shenk J at 822: 'Here the defendant's letterhead was printed on its stationery at some earlier time for a purpose unconnected with the transaction in suit.' Carter J gave a strong dissenting judgment in this case, which has much to recommend it.

with the statute) (1922); *Mesibov, Glinert & Levy, Inc. v Cohen Bros. Mfg. Co. Inc.*, 245 N.Y. 305, 157 N.E. 148 (no proof of intent is demonstrated when a paper has the name of a firm printed at the top but is not signed) (1927); *Reich v Helen Harper, Inc.*, 3 UCC Rep.Serv. 1048, 1966 WL 8838 (N.Y.City Civ.Ct.) (sales confirmation sent on stationery imprinted with the name of the seller's agent upon which the name of the seller's principal was handwritten was signed within the meaning of the UCC) (1966).

60 Federal 3rd circuit: *Associated Hardware Supply Co. v The Big Wheel Distributing Company*, 355 F.2d 114 (1966).

Federal 7th circuit: *Monetti, S.P.A. v Anchor Hocking Corporation*, 931 F.2d 1178 (7th Cir. 1991).

Connecticut: *Merrill Lynch, Pierce, Fenner & Smith, Inc. v Cole*, 189 Conn. 518, 457 A.2d 656 (Conn. 1983).

Georgia (1974): *Evans v Moore*, 131 Ga.App. 169, 205 S.E.2d 507; *Troutt v Nash AMC/Jeep, Inc.*, 157 Ga.App. 399, 278 S.E.2d 54 (the seller's standard printed form with the seller's company name, address and other information on the letterhead amounted to a signature) (1981).

Indiana: *Owen d/b/a Clark's Greenhouse and Clark's Greenhouse, Inc. v The Kroeger Company*, 936 F.Supp. 579 (S.D.Ind. 1996), 31 UCC Rep.Serv.2d 56.

Illinois: *Automotive Spares Corp. v Archer Bearings Company*, 382 F.Supp. 513 (1974) Bauer J at 515: 'This Court recognizes the need to use common sense and commercial experience in regards to this signature question. Often times merchants exchange documents which control the transaction that do not bear their signature.'

Maryland: *Drury v Young*, 58 Md. 546, 1882 WL 4502 (Md.), 42 Am.Rep. 343.

Michigan: *Benedict Manufacturing Co. v Aeroquip Corp.* 2004 WL 1532280, 53 UCC Rep.Serv.2d 888; *MFS & Company, LLC v Caterpillar, Inc.*, 2011 WL 4693897, 75 UCC Rep.Serv.2d 743.

Mississippi: *Dawkins and Company v L & L Planting Company*, 602 So.2d 838 (Miss. 1992) (a letter on the buyer's letterhead with the name of the sender typewritten at the bottom of the document was a sufficient signing to meet the merchant's exception to the Statute of Frauds).

New Jersey: *First Valley Leasing, Inc. v Goushy*, 795 F.Supp. 693 (D.N.J. 1992).

New York (1980): *B & R Textile Corp. v Domino Textiles, Inc.*, 77 A.D.2d 539, 430 N.Y.S.2d 89, 29 UCC Rep.Serv. 396.

Ohio: *Alarm Device Manufacturing Company v Arnold Industries, Inc.*, 65 Ohio App.2d 256, Ohio App., 417 N.E.2d 1284 (the letterhead on the seller's invoice was sufficient to satisfy the Statute of Frauds) (1979).

Texas: *Cox Engineering, Inc. v Funston Machine and Supply Company*, 749 S.W.2d 508 (Tex.App. 1988), 6 UCC Rep.Serv.2d 1399.

61 Kentucky: *Lamaster v Wilkerson*, 143 Ky. 226, 136 S.W. 217 (trustees caused their names to be printed on a notice prepared by them of the time and place of holding an election to issue bonds: the printed names were sufficient providing the trustees had authorized the printing of their names and had adopted them as their legal signatures) (1911).

Massachusetts: *Henshaw v Foster*, 9 Pick. 318, 26 Mass. 312, 1830 WL 25334 (Mass.) (in the election of the governor, votes may be printed).

New Jersey: *Matthews v Deane*, 201 N.J.Super. 583, 493 A.2d 632 (names printed on recall petitions are valid) (1984).

62 92 Cal.App.2d 157, 206 P.2d 676.

63 33 Cal.2d 814 (Cal. 1949), 205 P.2d 1025.

The use of a lithographed name

The use of printed forms to reduce wasted time is an accepted way of doing business. However, there are occasions when a manuscript signature is required under statute, more particularly with respect to the rules governing the running of a firm of solicitors. In the case of *R v Cowper (Fitzroy)*,[64] the name of the firm of solicitors was lithographed in bulk onto a county court bill of particulars. Spaces were left blank to fill in the form as necessary. A claim was made in respect of a debt and costs. At the hearing, the registrar refused an order for costs because the solicitors had not signed the particulars in accordance with the County Court Rules, 1889, order VI, r 10. The matter was then heard before the Divisional Court, which upheld the decision of the registrar. An appeal was subsequently heard in the Court of Appeal. Lord Esher pointed out that the name of a firm was included on the particulars to ensure the court may control its officers, and asked, at 535, 'If that was the object, how is it affected by the objection, that the name appears in a lithograph form?' and concluded that if the forms were misused, such misuse would inevitably be found out and punished. Further, he went on to demonstrate the reason for the rule at 535:

> The whole object of the rule seems to me to be to get the document authenticated as coming from a solicitor's office, and if the solicitor has authorized the issue of the lithograph form that object is attained. He means it to be his signature and sends it forth as his, and that seems to me sufficient compliance with the Act.

However, Fry LJ disagreed with Lord Esher. He thought that blank forms that can be filled up at any time did not offer any guarantee that the solicitor or a person authorized to act on their behalf had given their personal attention to a particular form. Also, and more compellingly, he argued, at 536, that 'the signature required is intended to be something to authenticate the particulars and the accuracy of the copies, and to make the solicitor responsible for them as an officer of the Court'. Thus attempts by solicitors to ease the burden of filling in forms has not always met with agreement from the bench, and in this case, because the members of the Court of Appeal did not agree, the decision of the Divisional Court was not changed. In comparison, a lithographed name on bonds has been held to be a valid signature in the United States, although the position would not be any different in England and Wales.[65]

The use of a rubber stamp

An early record of the use of a stamp, although not made with rubber, is that of the signature of a monarch from the Tudor period in England. Apparently the signet of Mary Tudor occurs with a stamp signature of the queen, of which more than

---

64 (1890) 24 QBD 533, [1890] 2 WLUK 7, (1890) 59 LJKB (NS) 265, CA, on appeal from *R v Cowper (Fitzroy)* (1889) 24 QBD 60, [1889] 12 WLUK 4.
65 California: *Hewel v Hogin*, 3 Cal.App. 248, 84 P. 1002 (the lithographic signatures of a secretary of an irrigation district were sufficient evidence of his signature to the bonds) (1906).

Missouri: *McKee v Vernon County*, 3 Dill. 210, 16 F.Cas. 188, No. 8851 (railroad bonds were valid where the signature of the presiding justice and clerk of the county were lithographed on the bond) (1874).

Mississippi: *Town Council of Lexington v Union National Bank*, 75 Miss. 1, 22 So. 291 (railroad bonds were valid with the signature of the clerk of the council lithographed on the bond) (1897).

twenty specimens appear on signet warrants. Also, there are examples of rubber stamps being used instead of seals in the nineteenth century by various sheriffs for official documents.[66] From the case law in relation to rubber stamps, it is generally, if reluctantly in some instances, accepted that a rubber stamp is capable of being accepted as a form of signature, providing the stamp is used with the authority of the person whose signature it is: for instance, in *Macdonald v Sun Life Assurance Company of Canada*[67] a medical expert retained by the defence was not permitted to testify after he stated that his signature stamp had been affixed to a medical report without his authority. The question of his signature arose when it became clear that the report he referred to during his testimony differed substantially from the one served on the plaintiff and filed with the court. The court did not consider any relevant legislation, but determined the issue on the basis of existing principles.

Wills

The case of *Jenkins v Gainsford and Thring*[68] illustrates the problems that people suffering from ataxia encounter, and what measures they take to resolve them. Towards the end of his life, John Jenkins had great difficulty in writing and signing his name, so he had an engraving of his signature made. Thereafter, when he was required to sign a letter or other document, he would direct his amanuensis to affix an impression of his name to the document by using the engraving. Mr Jenkins left a will and executed two codicils. An affidavit by his amanuensis accompanied the codicils, stating the manner in which they were executed: he was ordered and directed by the testator to affix the signature to the codicil using the engraving, in the presence of the other subscribing witness. After the signature was affixed, the testator placed his hand on the codicil and acknowledged the signature as his own and said the codicil was to be a codicil to his will. The two witnesses then attested and subscribed the codicil. The same procedure was followed on both occasions. Sir C Cresswell held that the codicils were duly executed. He observed that a testator has sufficiently signed by making their mark, and went on to note at 96:

> Now, whether the mark is made by a pen or by some other instrument cannot make any difference, neither can it in reason make a difference that a fac-simile of the whole name was impressed on the will instead of a mere mark or X.

The instrument or stamp was intended to stand for and represent the signature of the testator. The form the signature took was not relevant, providing the evidence surrounding the affixing of the stamp went to show that the testator intended to be bound by the content of the codicils.[69]

However, in Scotland the use of a stamp on a will is not acceptable in accordance with the provisions of Statute 1540, chapter 117. In *Stirling Stuart v Stirling Crawfurd's*

---

66 Barnes and Hector, *Guide to Seals*, 47 notes 2 and 52; articles that the reader might find of interest are Leonard W. Labaree and Robert E. Moody, 'The Seal of the Privy Council' (1928) 43 (170) The English Historical Review 190 and Clive Holmes, 'John Lisle, Lord Commissioner of the Great Seal, and the last months of the Cromwellian Protectorate' (2007) 122(498) The English Historical Review 918.
67 [2006] OJ No 4428 (Sup Ct) (QL), 2006 CanLII 41669 (ON SC).
68 (1863) 3 Sw & Tr 93; 164 ER 1208, (1862–63) 11 WR 854.
69 For almost identical facts where the deceased could no longer write because of arthritis and a stroke, see *Phillips v Najar*, 901 S.W.2d 561 (Tex.App.-El Paso 1995).

Trustees,[70] the testator signed a second deed by means of a stamp he was in the habit of using because he suffered from scrivener's palsy, and had great difficulty with writing.

Voting

The case of *Bennett v Brumfitt*[71] was brought under s17 of the Parliamentary Voters Registration Act 1843 before the Court of Common Pleas. The usual signature of William Brumfitt was engraved in facsimile and made into a stamp, which was subsequently used to sign a notice of objection. Bovill CJ observed at 31:

> The ordinary mode of affixing a signature to a document is not by the hand alone, but by the hand coupled with some instrument, such as a pen or pencil. I see no distinction between using a pen or a pencil and using a stamp, where the impression is put upon the paper by the proper hand of the party signing.

It is the personal act of the signatory that is relevant. Byles and Willes JJ agreed, and as to the genuineness of a signature, Keating J could not see why a document 'is better authenticated by a signature by means of a pen than by means of an impression of a stamp affixed by the party's own hand'.[72]

Judicial use

The development of technology permits actions that are repetitive in nature to be less onerous in their execution. Thus the use of a rubber stamp can alleviate the requirement that a manuscript signature be affixed to numerous documents by the same person in circumstances where the intention is to authenticate a document. Changes in technology included the adoption of stamps in the courts. In *Blades v Lawrence*,[73] a case was transferred to the City of London court by the order of a Master. The order was, in the words of Blackburn J, issued in the ordinary way 'according to the practice long established at Judge's Chambers, by the clerk of the judge, having on it the signature of the judge, stamped by the clerk'.[74] The judge in the London court inquired into the circumstances under which the order was made, and because the judge had not signed the order, he refused to hear the case and ordered the entry to be struck out. It was unanimously held by Cockburn CJ, Blackburn, Quain and Archibald JJ that such an order was properly authenticated and it was not for the judge of the London court, in the words of Cockburn CJ, 'to determine the validity or invalidity of the order bearing the proper authentication on its face'.[75] Where it was doubted that the order was genuine, the judge should have applied to a superior court to set the order aside. In this instance, the judge was ordered to pay the costs of the case.

---

70 (1885) 12 R. 610.
71 (1867–68) 3 LRCP 28.
72 (1867–68) 3 LRCP 28 at 32.
73 (1873–74) 9 LRQB 374, (1874) 43 LJR QB 133.
74 (1873–74) 9 LRQB 374 at 377.
75 (1873–74) 9 LRQB 374 at 376.

Consideration was given to the judicial use of rubber stamps in Ireland in the case of *The State v His Honour Judge P. J. Roe*,[76] where it was determined that a justice of the peace may sign a committal warrant by means of a rubber stamp. Gavan Duffy P said, at 186–187:

> As to the rubber stamps, if one man may sign by a mark, another may use a rubber facsimile as a signature; but, where the device is questioned by a man entitled to call for proof, the affixing of the stamp by the Justice must be proved, either by the Justice himself or by another witness who can swear positively to the making by the Justice of the particular signature questioned; and that may not be easy evidence for a Court clerk to give, if a Justice makes a habit of stamping his name on a sheaf of documents at one time. If the fact be that pressure of work makes the use of a rubber stamp a necessity, or almost a necessity, for a very busy Justice, one would expect to see the need expressly recognised in the code, with stringent rules for the safe custody of the stamp and a peremptory veto upon any delegation of its use to a clerk or any other person.

The acceptance of the use of a rubber stamp in legal proceedings is also illustrated in the Canadian case of *R v Burton*,[77] in which an informant affixed a facsimile signature to an information by means of a rubber stamp, which in turn was sworn before a justice of the peace, who signed the information with a manuscript signature. The information was held to be a sufficient signature in absence of proof that the officer who signed the jurat failed to comply with the duties imposed upon him. In reaching his decision, Lacourciere J observed, at 387:

> In my opinion the use of a rubber stamp signature by the informant is a practice that should be discouraged and indeed deprecated, as it detracts from the solemnity of an important step in the machinery of law, and may give rise to public suspicion that the officer taking the oath has done less than his duty. The partially stamped information, however, is not a nullity, in the absence of proof that the officer who signed the jurat failed to comply with the requirements set out above.

In comparison, an Ontario Court of Appeal held in the case of *R v Welsford, Re*[78] that an information charging an accused with a summary conviction offence under a provincial statute was a nullity if the jurat bore a facsimile rubber stamp signature of the justice of the peace.

Statute of Frauds

In *McDonald v John Twiname Ltd*[79] the plaintiff entered into an apprenticeship with the company, but an authorized representative from the company failed to sign the agreement. The name of the company was stamped on the document with a rubber stamp. In this instance, Evershed MR and Birkett LJ agreed that not only had the

---

76 [1951] IR 172.
77 [1970] 3 CCC 381, [1970] 2 OR 512, 8 CRNS 269 (Ont HCJ).
78 [1967] 2 OR 496, [1968] 1 CCC 1, 2 CRNS 5.
79 [1953] 2 QB 304, [1953] 3 WLR 347, [1953] 2 All ER 589, [1953] 6 WLUK 103, (1953) 97 SJ 505, [1953] CLY 1758.

document been signed by the company, but there was also sufficient evidence to show they had adopted, acted upon and affirmed the existence of the agreement.

Ecclesiastical use

The ecclesiastical use of rubber stamps is demonstrated in *De Beauvais v Green*,[80] where the bishop of Gloucester issued an order to the new incumbent to pay for repairs. One of the points raised in argument was that the bishop failed to sign the relevant order in triplicate in his own hand, as required by ss35 and 60 of the Ecclesiastical Dilapidations Act 1871, but authorized the use of a stamp for this purpose. It was held that the order by the bishop was sufficient in form to satisfy the requirements of the relevant sections.

Solicitors Act 1932

Solicitors, in the normal course of events, are required to sign bills of costs. In the case of *Goodman v J Eban Limited*,[81] a sole practitioner sought to recover for professional services provided to the defendant company. The solicitor affixed his name to the bill by means of a rubber stamp. The solicitor sent a bill of costs to the defendants, which was accompanied by a letter which ended in the words typewritten at the bottom of the letter 'Yours faithfully, Goodman, Monroe & Company'. Below the name, the solicitor affixed a facsimile of his signature by means of a rubber stamp. The defendants refused to pay the solicitor because the bill of costs did not satisfy the requirements of s65(2)(i) of the Solicitors Act 1932. It was held, with Denning LJ dissenting, that the bill had been signed for the purposes of s65, although, as Evershed MR observed at 554, 'as a matter of good practice, the "signature" of a bill of costs, or of a letter enclosing such a bill, by means of a rubber stamp seems to me in general undesirable'. He went on to comment that the purpose of the statute was to impose a personal responsibility for any bill of costs delivered, and the client was to have the assurance by means of personal authentication that the bill was a proper bill.[82] Romer LJ noted that the rubber stamp did not, on the face of it, constitute a signature,[83] although he accepted that when the matter was considered in the light of authority and the function that a signature was intended to perform, the conclusion must be that the rubber stamp did constitute a signature. He also concluded that a repetition of the name of the firm under the typewritten name would be otiose if it was only to repeat the typed name of

---

80 (1905–06) 22 TLR 816.
81 [1954] 1 QB 550, [1954] 2 WLR 581, [1954] 1 All ER 763, [1954] 3 WLUK 22, (1954) 98 SJ 214, [1954] CLY 3173.
82 The signature of a lawyer on a document usually indicates that the document has been read by that lawyer, as noted in the litigation following foreclosure claims as a result of the banking crisis in 2008, for which see *November Oversight Report* [Submitted under Section 125(b)(1) of Title 1 of the Emergency Economic Stabilization Act of 2008, Pub. L. No. 110343 Examining the Consequences of Mortgage Irregularities for Financial Stability and Foreclosure Mitigation] (Congressional Oversight Panel, 16 November 2010), http://cybercemetery.unt.edu/archive/cop/20110402010313/http://cop.senate.gov/documents/cop-111610-report.pdf; Office of the Inspector General US Department of Housing and Urban Development, *Bank of America Corporation Foreclosure and Claims Process Review Charlotte, NC* (Memorandum No. 2012FW1802, 12 March 2012), available at https://www.hudoig.gov/sites/default/files/Audit_Reports/2012-FW-1802.pdf; *In Re Hill*, 437 B.R. 503 (Bankr. W.D. Pa. 2010).
83 [1954] 1 QB 550 at 563.

the firm. It was plain that Mr Goodman intended the rubber stamp to 'be regarded as a signature for the purpose of authenticating the letter'.[84] Should the client doubt its authenticity, all they had to do was ask Mr Goodman, by telephone or letter.[85] Romer LJ might have also adopted, had he been aware of it, the reasoning of Clay J in the 1934 Kentucky case of *Wurts v Newsome*,[86] where a judge signed ballots by means of a rubber stamp. Clay J stated, at 450:

> The opportunities for fraud when a rubber stamp is used are no greater than the opportunities for fraud by forgery. It would be just as difficult to ascertain that the ballots had not been signed, and have a rubber stamp prepared, as it would be to employ one to imitate the signature of the judge who failed to sign. Besides, the statute, though designed to prevent fraud, has operated in several instances to defeat the popular will. In numerous contests that have come before this court, the successful candidate has lost by the failure of one of the judges, either through ignorance, mistake, or fraud to sign the ballots. In the circumstances we are not inclined to go further and adopt a construction so technical as to make the situation even worse. A rubber stamp identifies the ballot just as clearly as the written signature of the judge. If not placed on the ballot either by him, or someone else in his presence, and at his direction while the election is being conducted, that may be shown in a context just as it may be shown that the written signature appearing on the ballot was not his act. We therefore conclude that the signing of the ballots by a rubber stamp was a substantial compliance with the statute, and that all the ballots so signed should have been counted.

Dissenting, Denning LJ suggested that a person must make their mark, whatever the format, by themselves. In discussing the way in which rubber stamps were used, he introduced extraneous opinion to support his assertion, at 561, which was no more than prejudice and irrelevant to the matter being dealt with: 'This is such a common knowledge that a "rubber stamp" is contemptuously used to denote the thoughtless impress of an automaton, in contrast to the reasoned attention of a sensible person.' He overlooked several points. A rubber stamp is used to sign hundreds of letters or forms for convenience and saving in labour, as the case law illustrates, rather than the contemptuous use by a thoughtless automaton, the purpose of which is different to a solicitor's bill. Also, he clearly did not appreciate – and if he did, did not acknowledge – the fact that some people do not have the ability to sign documents. The issue was not the widespread use of rubber stamps in various other activities. In this judgment, Denning LJ refused to distinguish between the form a signature took and the function it was to perform, which has been the main thrust of judicial decision-making over the past two hundred years. Interestingly, the use of a stamp by judges and bishops during the nineteenth century was not raised or discussed in this case. If Denning LJ thought the personal signature of a solicitor was so necessary on a bill of costs, it may be equally as desirable when a judge orders a case to be transferred to another court, as in *Blades v Lawrence*.[87]

The decisions from other jurisdictions, together with the rationale articulated for accepting rubber stamps, also provide an instructive counterpoint to the comments by Denning LJ. In Canada, the judgment in *Goodman v J Eban Limited* was discussed in *R v*

---

84 [1954] 1 QB 550 at 564.
85 [1954] 1 QB 550 at 563–564.
86 253 Ky. 38, 68 S.W.2d 448.
87 (1873–74) 9 LRQB 374, (1874) 43 LJR QB 133.

Burton,[88] where an informant affixed a facsimile signature to an information by means of a rubber stamp; this was held to be a sufficient signature in the absence of proof that the officer who signed the jurat failed to comply with the duties imposed upon him. In the 1976 North Carolina case of *State of North Carolina v Watts*,[89] the mechanical reproduction of the name of an authorized officer placed on a public record of the Division of Motor Vehicles was held to be properly authenticated where the officer intended to adopt the mechanical reproduction as his signature. Branch J indicated, at 392, why the physical reality of the mechanical means of rendering a signature had become relevant:

> The purpose of authentication and certification of records is to avoid the inconvenience and sometimes the impossibility of producing original public documents in court. Obviously the admission of certified records tends to expedite the trial of cases. It is just as obvious that to require the manual signing of every record certified from the Division of Motor Vehicles would be extremely time-consuming and expensive.

Branch J's comments were reinforced by Hallet J in *Re United Canso Oil & Gas Ltd*,[90] where proxy forms submitted with a facsimile or mechanically rendered signature were considered to be sufficient. Hallett J explained the rationale at 289 paragraph 17:

> Today's business could not be conducted if stamped signatures were not recognized as legally binding. The affixing of a stamp conveys the intention to be bound by the document so executed just as effectively as the manual writing of a signature by hand. I would point out that no one questions the validity of millions of payroll cheques signed by facsimile signatures.

He also addressed the fallacious argument that one form of signature was more prone to fraud than any other at 305 paragraph 64:

> In my opinion, in view of the obvious opportunities for fraud with respect to votes to be cast by registered shareholders where a bare signature is normally accepted, I cannot see any reason to differentiate between the degree of proof required by a chairman to be satisfied that a proxy has actually been executed by the registered individual shareholder (the degree of proof being virtually nothing) and the degree of proof urged upon the court by the Buckley group with respect to proxy voting of brokers for their clients. In the absence of evidence that there was no authority for the execution of proxies by brokers by facsimile signature, the proxy vote should be accepted and counted as is apparently the practice. To conclude otherwise, the chairman is presuming dishonesty on the part of the brokers who tendered the proxies on behalf of their clients. In the absence of evidence, such a conclusion is unwarranted.

Administrative use

The inconvenience of affixing a manuscript signature to documents was also tested in administrative proceedings in the case of *British Estate Investment Society Ltd*

---

88 [1970] 3 CCC 381, [1970] 2 OR 512, 8 CRNS 269 (Ont HCJ); in *R v Blumes*, 2002 BCPC 45 (CanLII), it was not possible to determine whether the signature was an original signature, rubber stamp or facsimile signature; see also *R v Pearce*, 2000 BCSC 0376; *R v Parkinson*, [2002] OJ No 5478 (Ct J) (QL).
89   289 N.C. 445, 222 S.E.2d 389.
90   (1980) 12 BLR 130, 76 APR 282, 41 NSR (2d) 282 (TD).

v Jackson (H M Inspector of Taxes),[91] where an Additional Commissioner personally affixed his signature to certificates of authenticity by using a rubber stamp. The Additional Commissioner or the Clerk to the Commissioners retained the rubber stamp. Danckwerts J rejected all of the arguments by British Estate, and on the matter of the stamped signature he observed:

> Of course, this is a case, if ever there was a case, in which the signing by means of a stamped signature is proper, because everybody knows that Commissioners of this kind have to deal with numerous documents, and it is an onerous duty if they have to be signed by the writing of the Commissioner himself.[92]

In the contemporaneous case of *Lazarus Estates Ltd v Beasley*,[93] documents in the form prescribed by the Housing Repairs and Rents Act 1954 were signed with the name of the company by means of a rubber stamp. No objection was taken as to the validity of the signature in the county court, and the matter could not be addressed on appeal. However, Denning LJ could not resist commenting, at 710, that:

> The statutory forms require the documents to be 'signed' by the landlord, but the only signature on these documents (if such it can be called) was a rubber stamp 'Lazarus Estates Ltd.' without anything to verify it. There was no signature of a secretary or of any person at all on behalf of the company. There was nothing to indicate who affixed the rubber stamp. It has been held in this court that a private person can sign a document by impressing a rubber stamp with his own facsimile signature on it: *Goodman v J Eban Limited* [[1954] 1 QB 550; [1954] 2 WLR 581; [1954] 1 All ER 763, CA], but it has not yet been held that a company can sign by its printed name affixed with a rubber stamp.

This comment by Lord Denning was not to the point, and in the light of the extensive case law relating to this topic, from both England and Wales and the United States, it may be safe to indicate that Lord Denning's remarks on the topic are irrelevant. Of interest is the case of *Fitzpatrick v Secretary of State for the Environment and Epping Forest DC*,[94] in which enforcement notices signed with the rubber stamp of the appropriate official bearing their facsimile signature were held to be valid in accordance with the provisions of s234(2) of the Local Government Act 1972. The members of the Court of Appeal reached their decision without, it appears, reference to any relevant case law.[95]

United States of America

The use of rubber stamps as a means of authenticating documents in the United States has only been tempered with the need to ensure that the version of the signature in the form of an impression of a rubber stamp was used with the intent to authenticate the document. The range of uses to which rubber stamps have been put, and which judges have accepted with minor exceptions, include cheques

---

91 (1954–58) 37 Tax Cas 79, [1956] TR 397, 35 ATC 413, 50 R & IT 33.
92 (1954–58) 37 Tax Cas 79 at 86.
93 [1956] 1 QB 702, [1956] 2 WLR 502, [1956] 1 All ER 341, [1956] 1 WLUK 543, [1956] 100 SJ 131, [1956] CLY 7545.
94 [1990] 1 WLUK 107, [1990] 1 PLR 8, (1990) 154 LG Rev 72, [1990] CLY 4361a.
95 This is of interest, bearing in mind the comments by Buxton and BrookeLJJ in *Copeland v Smith* [2000] 1 WLR 1371, [2000] 1 All ER 457, [1999] 10 WLUK 381, [2000] CP Rep 14, (1999) 143 SJLB 276, Times, 20 October 1999, [1999] CLY 457.

(checks),[96] matters pertaining to the Fifth Amendment,[97] elections,[98] finance statements,[99] and when affixed to letters[100] and public documents,[101] but not

96   Pennsylvania: *Robb v The Pennsylvania Co. for Insurance on Lives and Granting Annuities*, 40 W.N.C. 129, 3 Pa.Super. 254, 1897 WL 3989 (Pa.Super. 1897) affirmed by 186 Pa. 456, 40 A. 969; for a dissenting opinion, see 186 Pa. 456, 41 A. 49.
97   Federal 2nd circuit: *Biegeleisen v Ross*, 158 F.3d 59 (2nd Cir. 1998) (a valid IRS levy based on a notice signed with a signature stamp rather than a manuscript signature did not violate the Due Process Clause of the Fifth Amendment).
98   Kentucky: *Wurts v Newsome*, 253 Ky. 38, 68 S.W.2d 448 (it was a valid signature where a judge signed ballots by means of a rubber stamp) (1934).
99   Colorado: *In the Matter of Colorado Mercantile Co.*, 299 F.Supp. 55 (1969) (a financing statement submitted with a stamped signature was acceptable, even though the requirement at the time of filing was for a manual signature).
Connecticut: *In re Bengston*, 1965 WL 8262 (Bankr.D.Conn.), 3UCC Rep.Serv. 283 (a name printed in ink – understood to mean stamped with a rubber stamp – on a standard form financing statement satisfied the requirement that the secured party signed the financing statement).
Texas: *Brooks v The State of Texas*, 599 S.W.2d 312 (a pen packet reflecting convictions for theft burglary where the facsimile signature of the clerk was affixed by means of a rubber stamp did not bar admission of the pen packet at the penalty stage) (1979).
Connecticut: *In re Deep River National Bank*, 73 Conn. 341, 47 A. 675 (the signature of Clinton B. Davis, affixed to a promissory note as 'D., Treasurer', was held to be a valid signature) (1900).
100 Federal 6th circuit: *National Accident Society v Spiro*, 78 F. 774, 24 C.C.A. 334 (the facsimile signature of an officer of the company affixed to a printed letterhead of the company was sufficiently proven) (1897).
Wisconsin: *Kocinski v The Home Insurance Company*, 154 Wis.2d 56, 452 N.W.2d 360 (Wis. 1990) (a facsimile signature stamped on a document with a rubber stamp satisfied the requirement that the document be subscribed).
101 Arizona: *Maricopa County v Osborn*, 60 Ariz. 290, 136 P.2d 270 (the facsimile signature of the treasurer applied by rubber stamp was sufficient for refunding bonds) (1943).
Carolina: *Smith v Greenville County*, 188 S.C. 349, 199 S.E. 416 (the signature of the county treasurer on a tax execution affixed with a rubber stamp by someone in his office was the signature of the treasurer) (1938).
Florida: *State v City of Fort Lauderdale*, 149 Fla. 177, 5 So.2d 263 (facsimile signatures affixed to city hospital revenue certificates and the attached coupons were valid) (1941).
New York: *Tenement House Department of City of New York v Weil*, 76 Misc. Rep. 273, 134 N.Y.S. 1062 (an order issued under the Tenement House Law containing a facsimile signature affixed by an official by means of a rubber stamp was valid) (1912); *Brooklyn City Railroad Company v City of New York*, 139 Misc. 691, 248 N.Y.S. 196 (a notice of claim with the signatures of an officer and of a notary public affixed to the document with a rubber stamp was sufficient) (1930).
North Dakota: *Andre v North Dakota State Highway Commissioner*, 295 N.W.2d 128 (a record of a speeding violation with the words 'STAT. FEE JUL 24 1979 THOMAS EWING' stamped on the back of the paper was adequate for the intended purpose of informing the State Highway Department of an admission or adjudication of a traffic violation) (1980); *State of North Dakota v Obrigewitch*, 356 N.W.2d 105, (N.D. 1984) (an order of suspension and driving record was valid where a rubber stamp was used to affix the signature of the director of the Driver's License Division of the State Highway Department).
Oklahoma: *Moss v Arnold*, 63 Okl.Cr. 343, 75 P. 491 (the facsimile signature of the chairman of the Board of County Commissioners applied by means of a rubber stamp was sufficient to authenticate requisitions) (1938); *State of Oklahoma ex rel. Independent School District Number One of Tulsa County v Williamson*, 352 P.2d 394 (Okla. 1960), 1960 OK 126 (the Uniform Facsimile Signature of Public Officials Act 1959 was valid and officials could use facsimile signatures on public bonds as a substitute for manuscript signatures as required by law).

receipts.[102] The judicial use of rubber stamps appears to have been widely taken up in various states, and although a federal court accepted that a search warrant signed with a rubber stamp by a magistrate was held to be valid in the seventh circuit case of *United States of America v Juarez*,[103] Tone CJ did not fully approve, commenting at 1114:

> Defendant also contends that the search warrant should be invalidated because the magistrate used a signature stamp instead of signing it personally. We do not approve the use of a signature stamp by a magistrate. Its use creates the appearance that the user lacks the sensitivity a federal judicial officer should have to the important values which the warrant is designed to protect.
>
> Nevertheless, in this case the magistrate testified unequivocally that he remembered placing the signature stamp on the warrant, and the District Court credited this testimony. We cannot say that it was clearly erroneous for the court to have done so. We therefore do not find that it was in error to refuse to declare the warrant invalid and thereby exclude the evidence seized pursuant to the warrant, despite our condemnation of the magistrate's practice.

At a state level, the use of rubber stamps has been widely accepted,[104] and Hood AJ indicated how widely rubber stamps were used in the 1943 Columbia case of *McGrady v*

Utah: *Salt Lake City v Hanson*, 19 Utah 2d 32, 425 P.2d 773 (the signatures of a police officer and city judge to a complaint, affixed by means of a rubber stamp, were sufficient) (1967).

102 Georgia: *Bell Bros. v Western & A. R. Co.*, 125 Ga. 510, 54 S.E. 532 (a freight receipt for a car containing cabbages signed by stencil with the name of the agent of the defendant company was not accepted because there was no proof that the agent signed the receipt, adopted the signature, or that it was his custom to sign his name to receipt by this type of stamp) (1906).

Massachusetts: *Boardman v Spooner*, 13 Allen 353, 95 Mass. 353, 1866 WL 5009 (Mass.), 90 Am.Dec. 196 (a bill of sale of goods bearing the purchaser's name stamped upon it was not sufficient proof to show that the stamp was adopted as a signature).

103 549 F.2d 1113 (1977).

Maine: *Mahoney v Ayoob*, 124 Me. 20, 125 A. 146, 37 A.L.R. 85 (where a disclosure commissioner endorsed a capias signed with his facsimile signature impressed with a rubber stamp, this was not a signature because the signature was not under his hand) (1924).

104 Florida: *State of Florida v Hickman*, Fla., 189 So.2d 254 (the facsimile signature of a justice of the peace affixed to a warrant by a rubber stamp was valid, even when affixed by the chief clerk under the authority of the justice) (1966).

Illinois: *Streff v Colteaux*, 64 Ill.App. 179, 1896 WL 2352 (Ill.App. 1 Dist.) (a declaration may be signed with the names of the plaintiff's attorneys by means of a rubber stamp) (1896); *People of the State of Illinois v Stephens*, 297 N.E.2d 224 (a search warrant signed by a magistrate with a rubber stamp was not invalid) (1973).

Iowa: *Loughren v B. F. Bonniwell & Co.*, 125 Iowa 518, 101 N.W. 287, 106 Am.St.Rep. 319 (the subscription by a justice with a rubber stamp bearing the facsimile of his signature was sufficient for a notice, even when carried out by another, but with his authority) (1904).

Massachusetts: *Wheeler v Lynde*, 1 Allen 402, 83 Mass. 402, 1861 WL 6171 (Mass.) (it was a signature where an attorney at law signed the back of a writ by means of a rubber stamp) (1861).

New Mexico: *Costilla Estates Development Co. v Mascarenas*, 33 N.M. 356, 267 P. 74 (the signature of a court clerk by means of a rubber stamp as a method of endorsement of filing papers was held sufficient) (1928).

Pennsylvania: *Commonwealth Department of Transportation v Ballard*, 17 Pa. Cmwlth. 310, 331 A.2d 578 (the signature of a traffic court judge by means of a rubber stamp was not inadmissible where the seal of the court was also applied to the record) (1975).

Munsey Trust Co.,[105] where the chief deputy clerk personally applied a facsimile representation of his signature to a summons. Hood AJ indicated the general use of the methods in his comments at 106: 'This practice was adopted many years ago and is a matter of great convenience since more than 4,000 landlord and tenant complaints are filed in the trial court each month.' The legal and practical position of rubber stamps was put into context by Lattimore J in the 1930 Texas case of *Stork v State*,[106] in which the facsimile signature of a justice of the peace affixed by rubber stamp to an affidavit and liquor search warrant was held to be a sufficient signing. Lattimore J considered a number of cases, and stated, at 735:

> The writer is of opinion that when it appears without question, as in this case, that the magistrate in person took the affidavits of those who swore to same, and also so issued the search warrant, and that to each he affixed his name, it would be a matter of no moment whether he so affixed said name by one stroke as by the use of a stencil or rubber stamp, or whether he sat down at a typewriter and wrote his name with same upon such document, or that he wrote it out in what we commonly call longhand, provided that in each such case the facts must allow the name to have been affixed by the officer himself, or under his immediate authority and direction and in his presence.

A stencil-pen

An interesting variation of technology for appending a copy of a manuscript signature was used in the case of *Whyte v Watt*,[107] before the Registration Appeal Court in Scotland. An objector signed a notice of objection using an instrument called a stencil-pen. The letters forming his signature were perforated upon a prepared wax skin, stretched on

---

Texas: *Ex parte Spencer*, 171 Tex.Cr.R. 339, 349 S.W.2d 727 (a complaint was valid where the complainant and the deputy clerk both affixed their signatures by means of a facsimile rubber stamp) (1961); *Ex parte Britton*, 382 S.W.2d 264 (a facsimile stamped signature of the governor on extradition papers did not affect the validity of the warrant) (1964); *Parsons v The State of Texas*, 429 S.W.2d 476 (a complaint was sufficiently signed with the facsimile signature of the complainant with a rubber stamp) (1968); *Estes v State*, 484 S.W.2d 711 (a facsimile signature applied to a document from the Department of Corrections by means of a rubber stamp was a sufficient signature) (1972); *Huff v The State of Texas*, 560 S.W.2d 652 (the facsimile signature of the county district clerk stamped on certified copies of a judgment and sentence was valid) (1978); *Paulus v The State of Texas*, 633 S.W.2d 827 (Tex.Crim.App. 1981) (there was no error when an indictment was signed with the facsimile signature of the foreman of a jury by means of a rubber stamp); *Benavides v State of Texas*, 763 S.W.2d 587 (Tex.App. – Corpus Christi 1988) (a penitentiary packet stamped with a rubber stamp producing a facsimile of an original signature was an acceptable means of signing legal documents); *Kemp v State of Texas*, 861 S.W.2d 44 (Tex.App. – Houston 14th Dist. 1993) (the use of a rubber stamp to produce a facsimile of a county judge's signature on a list of previous criminal records did not affect the authenticity of the signature); *In re Barber*, 982 S.W.2d 364 (Tex. 1998) (the signature of a judge affixed by a rubber stamp was a signature on a judgment, even when affixed to the document by an intermediate authority at the direction of the judge).

Utah: *State of Utah v Montague*, 671 P.2d 187 (Utah 1983) (clerk of the court affixing an imprint of the judge's signature with the authority of the judge to for the purpose of certifying the document as being a true original).

Wisconsin: *Dreutzer v Smith*, 56 Wis. 292, 14 N.W. 465 (a rubber stamp with a facsimile of the signature of the County Clerk affixed to a tax deed was considered to be writing the name) (1882).

105 32 A.2d 106.
106 114 Tex.Crim. 398, 23 S.W.2d 733.
107 (1893) 21 R. 165; see also *Henderson v Watt* (1893) 1 SLT 342.

a frame. He then placed the notice under the waxed skin and passed an inked roller over the waxed skin. As the ink from the roller passed through the perforations in the waxed skin, it produced the signature on the notice. Mr Watt formed the signature; no other person was employed in the operation. When letters or words have been formed on the waxed skin by the stencil-pen in this way, up to 100 sheets of paper – or more – can be placed successively under the waxed skin, and as the inked roller passes over the waxed skin, so the letter or words are produced on the sheet of paper immediately under the waxed skin. The validity of the signature was challenged, in that it did not comply with the provisions of s4 of 19 & 20 Victoria chapter 58, Registration of Burgh Voters (Scotland) Act 1856 in particular, according to forms 4 and 5 of schedule A. Kinnear, Trayner and Kincairney LL dismissed the appeal without calling on counsel for the respondent. They followed the judgment of the English court in the case of *Bennett v Brumfitt*,[108] and held that the provisions of the statute requiring that the objector should sign a notice of objection had been satisfied. It was noted that such a signature would not be sufficient to satisfy the conditions of the statute regulating the subscription and attestation of probative deeds, but that was not necessary in order to satisfy the requirements of the statute under construction. Kinnear L said, at 166–167:

> The word 'signed' is not a technical word but a word of ordinary language. Subscription is a method of signing. It is not the only method. We are therefore to consider whether the method of authentication described in the case can properly be called 'signing'. Now, upon that question, we have the advantage of a decision of the Court of Common Pleas, in the construction of a similar provision in the 6th of the Queen, chapter 18, which requires that a 'notice of objection shall be signed by the objector'. In *Bennett v Brumfitt*, L. R., 3 C. P. 28, the Court held that this requirement was satisfied although the objector had not subscribed the notice but had affixed his name to it by means of a stamp on which was engraved a facsimile of his ordinary signature. I cannot suppose that when the Legislature has employed the same language in a Scots Act as in a previous English Act, it intended to prescribe one method of authentication in England and another in Scotland, and I should be very slow to differ from the learned Judges in England as to the meaning of an ordinary word in the English language.

---

108 (1867–68) 3 LRCP 28.

7
Mechanical signatures

Signature machines

Machines for writing multiple copies of a signature have a long history. John Isaac Hawkins (1772–1855) is credited with inventing what is generally referred to as an autopen, known at the time as a pentagraph.[1] An 'autopen' featured in a case begun by the chef Gordon Ramsay, who took legal action against his father-in-law, Christopher Hutcheson, over a lease for a pub called the York & Albany in London. The lease was signed in 2007 for an annual rent of £640,000. Mr Ramsay's signature was affixed to the lease using a Ghostwriter Manual Feed Signature Machine. Mr Ramsay claimed that the signature was a forgery. Morgan J described how the machine worked at [75]:

> To use the machine, an operator needed a number code, to be tapped into the machine by use of a key pad, and a signature card. The signature card identified the signature which the machine would produce. It was also necessary to fit a pen to the machine. In this case, the pens which were used included a pen which produced the result of using a felt tip pen and another pen which gave the appearance of a pen with a fine knib being used. The felt tip signature was suitable for signing books or photographs and the fine knib pen was suitable for signing legal documents and cheques.

Mr Justice Morgan decided that because Mr Hutcheson was acting as an agent for Mr Ramsay at the time, he had acted within the authority conferred on him by Mr Ramsay, and he had not exceeded his authority. Mr Ramsay was bound by the guarantee in the lease of the premises.[2]

Mechanical marks by human action

The application of legal principles applies to new technology in the same way as it relates to more established ways of conducting business.

Typewriting

Once the typewriter had developed sufficiently to enable a typist to type faster than a human could write, the machine began to be widely used. An early example of litigation

---

1 Obituary of Mr John Isaac Hawkins, (1866) 25 Proceedings of the Institution of Civil Engineers, 512, http://www.icevirtuallibrary.com/doi/pdf/10.1680/imotp.1866.23204.
2 *Ramsay v Love* [2015] EWHC 65 (Ch), [2015] 1 WLUK 295.

respecting the value of a typed signature was a case involving a remonstrance in 1905 in Indiana, that of *Ardery v Smith*.³ In this case, an attorney had the authority to sign a remonstrance against the issue of a liquor licence for and on behalf of voters, and being afflicted with erysipelas in his right hand, he caused the names to be typed in his presence and under his supervision. It was held to be immaterial that the names were added by means of a typewriter. Roby J summed up the position at 841:

> In an opinion given in 1842 by William Wirt, then Attorney General, the question submitted being whether the Secretary of the Treasury was authorized by a statute requiring warrants to be drawn and signed by him to have his name impressed thereon by means of copper plate, the following language was used: 'There would be great difficulty in maintaining the proposition, as a legal one, that, when the law required signing, it means that it must be done with pen and ink. No book has laid down the proposition, or even given color to it. I believe that a signature made with straw dipped in blood would be equally valid and obligatory, and, if so, where is the legal restriction on the implement which the signer may use? If he may use one pen, why may he not use several – a polygraph, for example, or types, or a stamp? The law requires signing merely as an indication and proof of the parties' assent.' 1 Opinions of Attorneys General, 670. The quotation is an apt one, as applied to the facts now under consideration. The typewriter is a modern convenience. The signature made by it was in this case the signature of the attorney; the operator being in fact his agent, exactly as the keys and the types were his agents.

From an evidential point of view, the person whose name was typed on the document must adopt the typed version as their signature.⁴ Crane J illustrated the difficulty that arises in this regard in the 1911 New York case of *Landeker v Co-operative Bldg. Bank*,⁵ demonstrating that it is necessary to link the application of the typewritten name to proof that the name was typed with authority and intent.⁶

---

3   35 Ind.App. 94, 73 N.E. 840.
4   For Australia see *Neill v Hewens* (1953) 89 CLR 1; for the United States of America, see Federal, 10th circuit: *Roberts v Johnson*, 212 F.2d 672 (it must be proven to be intended to be the signature of the witness where a form designating a beneficiary is signed with a typewritten name) (1954); California: *Estate of Moore*, 92 Cal.App.2d 120, 206 P.2d 413 (a will signed with a typewritten name could not be considered to be signed in the absence of evidence to show it was typed by the testator or that it was typed in his presence and at his direction by another) (1949); Maine: *Maine League Federal Credit Union v Atlantic Motors*, 250 A.2d 497, 6 UUC Rep.Serv. 198 (there was no intent to adopt a typewritten name on a financing statement; it was only through inadvertence that the document was not signed with a manuscript signature) (1969); Massachusetts: *Andre v Ellison*, 324 Mass. 665 (1949) 88 N.E.2d 340; Missouri: *First Security Bank of Brookfield v Fastwich*, 612 S.W.2d 799 (Mo.App. 1981) (the burden of establishing the typed signature of a corporation arose when it was put in issue by a specific denial. The burden was on the party claiming under the signature, but he was aided by the presumption that it was genuine or authorized); in the Court of First Instance of Hong Kong in the case of *Shenzhen Tian He Jian Sang Electronic Holdings Company Limited v Hong Kong Jian Sang Electronics (Group) Limited* [2008] HKCFI 387, HCA 1587/2007, 9 May 2008, Hon Fung J held that it could not be inferred that an unsigned copy of a letter with the typed name of the second defendant was intended to be a signed copy addressed to the plaintiff.
5   130 N.Y.Supp. 780.
6   See also the 1911 Californian case of *Little v Union Oil Company of California*, 73 Cal.App. 612, 238 P. 1066; the Maryland case of *Cambridge, Inc. v The Goodyear Tire & Rubber Company*, 471

Interestingly, a number of cases dealing with typewritten signatures are of relatively recent origin, and it is to be wondered, when reading some of the reports, whether the points ought to have been taken at all, given the long and liberal history adopted by the common law in relation to the form a signature takes.[7] Examples include arbitration,[8] mechanics' lien,[9] Statute of Frauds,[10]

F.Supp. 1309 (1979) where a typewritten name on a lease did not bind where it was not intended to bind as a legal signature; and the 1926 Pennsylvania case of *Tabas v Emergency Fleet Corporation*, 9 F.2d 648 *affirmed United States Shipping Board Emergency Fleet Corporation v Tabas*, 22 F.2d 398 where the government of the United States was not deemed to have executed a contract because its name was typed on paper in the absence of evidence to show it had authorized or adopted such signature.

7   Although see the Maine case of *In re Carlstrom*, 3 UCC Rep.Serv. 766, 1966 WL 8962 (Bankr.D.Me.), where a typewritten name on a financing statement was not accepted as a signature. Note the astounding views of Conrad, Referee in Bankruptcy, negating the concept that a symbol can be considered a signature, and his hostile comments on the decision in *Benedict, Trustee in Bankruptcy of Lillian E. Hargrove d/b/a Hargrove Typesetting Services v Lebowitz*, 346 F.2d 120 (1965). For the absence of a manuscript signature on a typed letter with the name of the person typed below the space for a signature, and subsequently scanned and attached to an email, and where the typed name was sufficient, see the Massachusetts case of *Hamdi Halal Mkt. LLC v United States*, 947 F. Supp. 2d 159 (D. Mass. 2013).

8   Illinois: *Just Pants, an Illinois limited partnership v Wagner*, 617 N.E.2d 246 (Ill.App. 1 Dist. 1993) (the typewritten name of an arbitrator at the end of a memorandum of decision could serve to execute and give legal effect to the contents).

9   New Jersey: *J. D. Loizeaux Lumber Company v Davis*, 124 A.2d 593, 41 N.J. Super. 231 (the name of the plaintiff typed on a materialman's notice of intention was held to be intended to be a signing as well as to serve other functions disclosed by the printed material) (1956).

10   Federal, 9th circuit: *In the Matter of Save-On-Carpets of Arizona, Inc.*, 545 F.2d 1239 (1976) (a typewritten signature on a UCC financing statement satisfied the signature requirement of the Statute of Frauds).

Alaska: *A & G Construction Co., Inc. v Reid Brothers Logging Co., Inc.*, 547 P.2d 1207 (the name 'Glenn W. Reid' typed at the bottom of a letter was considered to be signed) (1976).

Florida: *Ashland Oil, Inc. v Pickard*, Fla., 269 So.2d 714 (the typed words on notepaper with the letterhead of the company and with the word 'Harold L. Slam, President' typed at the bottom was a signature) (1972).

Maryland (1967): *Dubrowin v Schremp*, 248 Md. 166, 235 A.2d 722.

Massachusetts: *Irving v Goodimate, Co.*, 320 Mas. 454, 70 N.E.2d 414, 171 A.L.R. 326 (the name of the employer typed at the end of a letter to an employee was a sufficient signature) (1946).

Minnesota: *Radke v Brendon*, 271 Minn. 35, 134 N.W.2d 887 (a prospective vendor's letter including the prospective purchaser's name and typewritten name of the vendor was tantamount to a written signature, given the intent) (1965).

Mississippi: *Dawkins and Company v L & L Planting Company*, 602 So.2d 838 (Miss. 1992) (a letter written on a buyer's letterhead including the typewritten name of the sender was a sufficient signing to meet the merchant's exception to the Statute of Frauds).

New York (1919): *Cohen v Wolgel*, 107 Misc. Rep. 505, 176 N.Y.S. 764 *affirmed* 191 A.D. 883, 180 NY.S. 933.

New Mexico: *Watson v Tom Growney Equipment, Inc.*, 721 P.2d 1302 (N.M. 1986) (a name typed on a purchase order was held to be a sufficient signature because the signatory had deliberately filled out other details on the order form).

Wisconsin (1912): *Garton Toy Co. v Buswell Lumber & Mfg. Co.*, 150 Wis. 341, 136 N.W. 147.

mortgages,[11] modification of a loan,[12] pleadings,[13] secured transactions,[14] bonds,[15] taxation[16] and wills.[17]

In New Zealand, this concept is called the 'authenticated signature fiction' and is illustrated by the case of *Bilsland v Terry*,[18] where an agreement for the sale of land had the names of both parties set out in the document, but it was signed only with the manuscript signature of one party. It was held to be a sufficient signing to satisfy s2 of the Contracts Enforcement Act 1956. Quilliam J commented, at 50:

> Upon the authority, therefore, of the cases I have cited I find that the agreement was a sufficient memorandum in writing to satisfy the Contracts Enforcement Act, and is binding on the parties. I should mention that it was contended by Mr Luck that the conclusion I was invited to draw upon the basis of the authorities I have cited was plainly wrong, and that if I were to adopt it I should be introducing into the realm of conveyancing a hazard which should not be there. I realize that the rule to which I have referred is probably unknown to

---

11 Federal 2nd circuit: *Benedict, Trustee in Bankruptcy of Lillian E. Hargrove d/b/a Hargrove Typesetting Services v Lebowitz*, 346 F.2d 120 (1965) (the insertion of the name in the body of a financing statement was held to be a sufficient signing. The intent to authenticate was established by the act of a secretary in typing his name at his direction and subsequently filing the statement).
12 Michigan: *Etts v Deutsche Bank National Trust Company*, 126 F.Supp.3d 889 (E.D.Mich. 2015).
13 Indiana: *City of Gary v Russell*, 123 Ind.App. 609, 112 N.E.2d 872 (a notice of claim was sufficiently signed when the plaintiff's name was typewritten at the end) (1953).
North Dakota: *Hagen v Gresby*, 159 N.W. 3, 34 N.D. 349, 5 L.R.A. 1917B, 281 (the typewritten name and address of an attorney on a summons was sufficient. The attorney, F. B. Lambert, had not written a summons with a manuscript signature since 1896) (1916).
14 Federal 4th circuit: *Calaway v Admiral Credit Corporation*, 407 F.2d 518 (a financing statement with a typed name was not invalid for lack of manuscript signature where a typewritten signature was provided) (1969).
Federal 5th circuit: *In the Matter of Bufkin Brothers, Inc.*, 757 F.2d 1573 (1985) (a secured creditor's typewritten corporate name on a continuation statement was sufficient to validate the statement).
Connecticut: *In re Horvath*, 1963 WL 8592 (Bankr.D.Conn.), 1UCC Rep.Serv. 624 (a typewritten name considered a signature) (1963).
Georgia: *Peoples Bank of Bartow County v Northwest Georgia Bank*, 139 Ga.App. 264, 228 S.E.2d 181 (the printed name of the bank on a financing statement served to reinforce a manuscript signature that was not easily identified) (1976).
15 Texas: *B. F. Bridges & Son v First Nat. Bank of Center*, 47 Tex.Civ.App. 454, 105 S.W. 1018 (a typed signature to a bond was sufficient if adopted) (1907).
16 Massachusetts: *Assessors of Boston v Neal*, 311 Mass. 192, 40 N.E.2d 893 (an application for abatement was inadvertently not signed with a manuscript signature, but it was accompanied by a letter signed by the Treasurer of the First People's Trust; it was held that the application signed with a typewriter was sufficient) (1942).
17 In the 1944 Texas case of *Zaruba v Schumaker*, 178 S.W.2d 542, a will written by the deceased on a typewriter with her typewritten name was held to be signed; compare the 1949 case in California of *Estate of Moore*, 92 Cal.App.2d 120, 206 P.2d 413 where a will signed with a typewritten name could not be considered to be signed in the absence of evidence to show it was typed by the testator or that it was typed in his presence and at his direction by another.
18 [1972] NZLR 43.

many conveyancers, but this alone is hardly a reason for not applying it where the facts render it applicable. The rule appears to be well established and I can see no reason why I should ignore it.

This decision was followed in *Short v Graeme Marsh Ltd*,[19] but not in *Carruthers v Whitaker*[20] (*Bilsland v Terry* was not referred to in this judgment). The *Bilsland v Terry* and *Short v Graeme Marsh Ltd* cases were later distinguished in *Stuart v McInnes*,[21] where a contract for the sale of land was held not to be enforceable where neither party had signed the agreement. Wilson J discussed the 'authenticated signature fiction' at 733–734:

> Although, over the years, the basis for the authenticated signature fiction seems to have changed somewhat, the line of cases in England which includes Tourret v Cripps, Evans v Hoare and Leeman v Stocks has now settled the law on this topic. From these cases it is clear that, in England, the principle applies if, and only if, these conditions obtain:
>
>> (1) the contract, or the memorandum containing the terms of contract, must have been prepared by the party sought to be charged, or by his agent duly authorised in that behalf, and must have that party's name written or printed on it.
>>
>> (2) It must be handed or sent by that party, or his authorised agent, to the other party for that party to sign.
>>
>> (3) It must be shown, either from the form of the document or from the surrounding circumstances, that it is not intended to be signed by anyone other than the party to whom it is sent and that, when signed by him, it shall constitute a complete and binding contract between the parties.
>
> I think the justification for the fiction is to be found in the last condition. Where the form of the memorandum or the surrounding circumstances show the intention that the contract shall be binding on both parties although not signed by the one who prepared it, the terms of the statute are not really applicable with reference to that one, so the fiction is introduced to meet the case. It is easy to see the justice of the result, but I confess to a regret that the solution found was to describe as a signature something that is not a signature and was never intended to be such. It might have been preferable to hold that such memoranda were outside the ambit of the statute in regard to the party whose signature was not contemplated as being necessary.

He went on to discuss the decisions in *Bilsland v Terry* and *Short v Graeme Marsh Ltd* at 734–735, which he declined to follow. The same decision was reached in *Van der Veeken v Watsons Farm (Pukepoto) Ltd*,[22] where a contract for the sale of property called for the signature of both parties, and the authenticated signature fiction was considered not relevant to the fact of this case; the decision in *Bilsland v Terry* was also distinguished. It seems the current position in New Zealand is governed by *TA Dellaca Ltd v PDL Industries Ltd*,[23] where the approaches taken in *Bilsland v Terry* and *Short v Graeme Marsh Ltd* were rejected. The members of the court favoured the approach taken by Wilson J in *Stuart v McInnes* and Beattie J in *Van der Veeken v*

19 [1974] 1 NZLR 722.
20 [1975] 2 NZLR 667.
21 [1974] 1 NZLR 729.
22 [1974] 2 NZLR 146.
23 [1992] 3 NZLR 88.

Watsons Farm (Pukepoto) Ltd. Tipping J commented, at 99: 'I agree with their observations that to go further than the approach summarised by Wilson J really amounts to an unacceptable judicial repeal of the Contracts Enforcement Act 1956. The authenticated signature fiction is itself quite a significant departure from the literal terms of the Act.'

In Canada, the use of a typed signature in combination with an authorized manuscript signature of a departmental lawyer was the issue in the case of *R v Fredericton Housing Limited*.[24] The question was whether the typewritten signature of the Deputy Attorney General of Canada was acceptable on a statement of claim, together with the manuscript signature of a lawyer in the department. The manuscript signature 'F. J Dubrule' was affixed to the statement of claim by a solicitor in the Tax Litigation Section of the Department of Justice, of which section Mr Dubrule was the director. It was held that the signature was the signature of Mr Dubrule. It was duly authorized by him, and the typed name 'D. S. Maxwell', when it was authenticated by the subscription of the signature of Mr Dubrule, became the signature of the Deputy Attorney General of Canada. Cattanach J made a useful observation, at 223, in discussing the difference between using a rubber stamp to affix a signature and a typewriter: 'If the typewritten name "D. S. Maxwell" is not "writing" (as I think it is) it is most certainly a mechanical method of affixing and I cannot distinguish in principle an affixing by keys striking a ribbon from a rubber stamp with ink on it.'

The members of the Court of Appeal in England and Wales had occasion to consider the requirement of a signature on a document for the sale of land in the case of *Firstpost Homes Ltd v Johnson*.[25] In this case a director of the company reached an oral agreement with Miriam Fletcher, the owner of land in Staffordshire, whereby she agreed to sell the land. A secretary typed a letter on 9 April 1993 for Mrs Fletcher to sign. Mrs Fletcher's address was typed on the top right-hand side of the letter and it was addressed to Mr Hale of Firstpost Homes Ltd, followed by the address of the company. The letter continued:

> Dear Geoff, re: Land and rear of Fulfen Farm, Burntwood Further to our recent discussions I now agree to sell you the above land shown on the enclosed plan which extends to 1564 acres in consideration of the sum of £1,000 (One thousand pounds) per acre. Yours sincerely.

Then there was a gap, and typed underneath this were the words 'M. Fletcher (Mrs)'. A plan, a copy of an Ordnance Survey plan showing the land in question, was attached to the letter by a paper clip. Mr Hale signed the plan at the foot. He delivered the letter to Mrs Fletcher on Friday 1 April 1993 and returned on Sunday 11 April. Mrs Fletcher signed the letter and the plan. She died on 12 May 1993. The personal representatives refused to conclude the contract for the sale of the land and the company sought specific performance.

---

24 [1973] FC 196, [1973] CTC 160.
25 [1995] 1 WLR 1567, [1995] 4 All ER 355, [1995] 7 WLUK 274, [1996] 1 EGLR 175, [1996] 13 EG 125, (1995) 92(28) LSG 30, (1995) 139 SJLB 187, [1995] NPC 135, Times, 14 August 1995, [1996] CLY 5025.

His Honour Judge Farrer QC refused the application. The appeal was dismissed. In giving a substantial judgment, Peter Gibson LJ pointed out the legislature had intended to make radical changes, and the changes were intended to simplify the law and avoid disputes when enacting the Law of Property (Miscellaneous Provisions) Act 1989. While the letter indicated Mrs Fletcher intended to sell the land, it was not clear that she intended to sell the land to the company. As a result, it was the letter, and not the plan, that formed the document of sale, and only Mrs Fletcher had signed this document. It was argued by the company that the typed name and address of the company were sufficient to show it was signed by the company. However, Peter Gibson LJ rejected this submission because it was based on previous authorities that in turn were based on earlier legislation, and not on the Law of Property (Miscellaneous Provisions) Act 1989. He considered it 'is an artificial use of language to describe the printing or the typing of the name of an addressee in the letter as the signature by the addressee when he has printed or typed the document'[26] and mentioned approvingly the comments made by Evershed MR and Denning LJ in *Goodman v J Eban Limited*.[27] Peter Gibson LJ no longer considered that the interpretation of the modern Act should be governed by the authorities in relation to the Statute of Frauds 1677 or s40 of the Law of Property Act 1925. It was decided that the company had not signed the letter, and there was, therefore, no contract in place, although this decision was 'limited to a case where the party whose signature is said to appear on a contract is only named as the address of a letter prepared by him'.[28] Hutchinson and Balcombe LJJ agreed with this analysis, and Balcombe LJ reiterated the point, at 1577 E, that the 'policy of the section is to avoid the possibility that one or other party may be able to go behind the document and introduce extrinsic evidence to establish a contract, which was undoubtedly a problem under the old law'.

The move from form to function has certainly been halted in the case of the sale of property.[29] It is the view of Julian Farrand and Alison Clarke that the decision in *Goodman* does not provide the support that Peter Gibson LJ claimed, and the decision in *Firstpost* 'not only involved flaws in law but also enabled an unmeritorious escape from contractual obligations'.[30]

Telegram

The development of telegraphy in the early nineteenth century brought about the same types of dispute that occur in the era of the Internet, and judges were required then, as now, to adapt old laws to new technologies. The telegram and its various technologies, including the telex, were widely used from the outset. The telegram is the first incarnation of the electronic signature. In *Godwin v Francis*,[31] an offer to buy a property was accepted by telegram. It was held that the telegram, together with other

---

26 [1995] 1 WLR 1567 at 1575 F-G.
27 [1954] 1 QB 550, [1954] 2 WLR 581, [1954] 1 All ER 763, [1954] 3 WLUK 22, (1954) 98 SJ 214, [1954] CLY 3173.
28 [1995] 1 WLR 1567 at 1576 E.
29 For signatures relating to the law of property, see Julian Farrand and Alison Clarke, *Emmet on Title* (Sweet & Maxwell, loose-leaf).
30 Farrand and Clarke, *Emmet on Title*, 2.041.
31 (1870) LR 5 CP 295, 22 LT Rep NS 338.

Mechanical signatures

correspondence, was sufficient to satisfy the Statute of Frauds, and the signature of the telegraph clerk was considered a sufficient signature. In response to the argument that the instructions for the sending of the telegram could not be a signature of the contract because the paper was a mere instruction to the telegraph clerk, Bovill CJ responded, at 301–302:

> Assuming that argument to be correct (though I am not prepared to adopt it), that would be instructions to the company to do that which in the ordinary course of their business is done. Now, the ordinary course of business is to transmit, to write out, an exact copy of that which is intended to be conveyed, and to forward it. The acceptance of the plaintiff's offer is in the body of the document. The telegraph clerk copies it, signs it, and sends it to the plaintiff, the name of the seller appearing thereon. A correspondence ensues between the parties on the footing that there had been a binding contract for the sale of the estate; and, if the defendant had authority, it is clear that what was done did constitute a binding contract. But, independently of that, I am prepared to hold that the mere telegram written out and signed in the way indicated by the telegraph clerk, if done with the authority of the vendors, would have been a sufficient signature within the Statute of Frauds.

It was necessary to resolve the distinction between the contents of the document containing the message to be sent and subsequently presented to the telegraph office, and the document received by the recipient. In this respect, Willes J observed, at 302–303 that:

> The message was left, signed by the defendant, at the office of the Telegraph Company. A copy was sent by the company to the plaintiff, and authenticated by them in the usual way. If the message so sent had been contained in a letter sent by post, there can be no doubt that would have been a sufficient contract to satisfy the statute. That is because the General Post Office has been held to be the common agent of the parties employing it.

Brett J also noted, at 303:

> I think there is evidence that the defendant, when he signed the instructions, intended that to operate as his signature to the contract, and that it constituted a binding contract signed by him, if he had authority to enter into it. Then, it was objected that the defendant's name appearing on the paper received by the plaintiff was insufficient, because the defendant had no power to delegate to the telegraph clerk an authority to sign his name. I think, however, it must be assumed as against him that he had authority to delegate to the clerk the power to sign for him, and that the signature so placed was binding upon him.

A number of cases concerning the exchange of telegrams were dealt with in a similar way as some forms of electronic signature are dealt with today: the point was not raised in argument, and therefore the issue of the efficacy of the signature was not challenged, inferring an acceptance of the proof of intent of the parties in the case.[32]

---

32 In *Henkel v Pape* (1870) 6 L.R.Exch. 7 and *L. Roth and Co. (Limited) v Taysen, Townsend, and Co.* (1896–97) 12 TLR 211 CA contracts were formed by exchange of telegrams; the signature point was not raised in either case, but it can be inferred that it was accepted; in *Sadgrove v Bryden* [1907] 1 Ch 318, the words 'Consent, Shaw' sent by cablegram, which was, in turn, stamped with a 10 shilling stamp as power of attorney, was held sufficient to validate a form of proxy signed in advance but not dated in accordance with the provisions of s80 of the Stamp Act 1891; in *Behnke v Bed Shipping Co* [1927] 1 KB 649 a contract for the sale and purchase of a ship was conducted by letter, telegram and telephone, and

It is plain that the introduction of technology was not an excuse for preventing the application of legal principles to new technology. In *McBlain v Cross*,[33] it was held that the signature in a telegram was sufficient to come within the Statute of Frauds. Willes J was not going to let technology impede the way in which the law was interpreted, commenting, at 806, that 'If we did not hold such to be the law, the convenience which the modern invention of the electric telegraph has bestowed upon mankind would be in a great measure subverted'.

In 1886 it was determined that a person may provide authority to sign a name to a memorandum of association under the Companies Act 1862,[34] and Vaughan Williams J had the foresight to issue a novel form of order in the case of *In re English, Scottish, and Australian Chartered Bank.*[35] In this case, the principal business of the bank was in Australia, but it was ordered that the bank had to be wound up in England. A scheme of reconstruction was proposed, and Vaughan Williams J directed that meetings of shareholders and creditors be held to ascertain their wishes. The majority of the creditors were in Australia, and because of the need for speed, Vaughan Williams J made an entirely new form of order directing a form of proxy to be sent by the Official Receiver by telegraph to Australia, appointing specified persons to vote for or against the scheme at the meeting to be held in London. A number of objections were taken on the result of the vote in the meeting. One of the objections was that the judge had no power to order the Australian proxies to be communicated by telegram to the meeting. The proxies ought to have been produced at the meeting. It was held that the judge had the power under s91 of the Companies Act 1862, in combination with s2 of the Joint Stock Companies Arrangement Act 1870, to direct the particulars of the Australian proxies to be communicated by telegraph, and there was no need for the proxies to be physically produced at the meeting. Lindley LJ commented, at 410: 'Now, that is an entirely new form of order. I need hardly say that it is adapted to the necessities of the time – it is ingeniously using the improved methods of communication by telegraph, which it would be folly to shut out and not use if you can do it.' Smith LJ said, at 417:

> I wish to add a few remarks upon a point which for the first time arises in this case, that is as to whether or not the electric telegraph can be made use of to carry out what was eminently needed, and indeed was absolutely necessary to do justice in this case.

Telegrams were as widely used in South Africa[36] and the United States of America as in any other jurisdiction. In 1869 the process involved in sending and receiving a telegram was outlined by Sargent J in the New Hampshire case of *Howley v Whipple.*[37] In this instance, the decision centred on the requirements to provide for the proper evidential foundation necessary in adducing evidence of a telegram into proceedings. In addition, it also

---

it was held that a name added to a telegram was a signature where it was adopted or recognized by the party to be charged.
33   (1872) LT 804.
34   *In re Whitley Partners Callan's Case* (1886) 55 LJCh (NS) 540.
35   [1893] 3 Ch 385.
36   *Hersch v Nel*, 1948 (3) SA 686 (AD); in *Luttig v Jacobs*, 1951 (4) SA 563 (OPD) the legal effect of the signature was not discussed; *Balzun v O'Hara* [1964] 3 All SA 368 (T).
37   48 N.H. 487 (1869).

followed that telegrams may constitute an adequate memorandum of the contract, and a contract could be construed by reference to several letters and telegrams.[38] The use of telegrams covered a range of situations, including bills,[39] judicial use[40] and the Statute of Frauds.[41] Generally, members of the judiciary took a robust view of telegrams, as illustrated in the 1912 Missouri case of *Leesley Bros. v A. Rebori Fruit Co.*,[42] where it was held that an exchange of two telegrams between the parties to buy and sell a carload of onion sets was held to be in substantial compliance with the Statute of Frauds. Nixon PJ remarked at 142: 'to hold otherwise would certainly embarrass present business methods and increase the expense and impair the usefulness of the telegraph as a necessary instrumentality in modern commerce.' This view was shared by Wolff,

---

38 Florida (1920): *Meek v Briggs*, 80 Fla. 487, 86 So. 271.

39 Kentucky (1918): *Selma Savings Bank v Webster County Bank*, 206 S.W. 870, 182 Ky. 604, 2 A.L.R. 1136.

40 Kentucky: *Blackburn v City of Paducah*, Ky., 441 S.W.2d 395 (a telegram sent by Judge John B. Blackburn containing his resignation from his post constituted a writing and was signed. The Board of Commissioners accepted the resignation and subsequently another police judge was appointed to fill the vacancy. When the appellant later attempted to act in this capacity, he was arrested) (1969). Clay, Commissioner, remarked, at 398: 'Perhaps we have belaboured the obvious too much. Here appellant selected the medium to the transmittal of his message, composed its content and authorized his signature thereto. It is difficult to understand how he can now question the legal efficacy of the written instrument he had drafted for the sole purpose of tendering his resignation.'

Oklahoma: *State ex rel. West v Breckinridge*, 34 Okla. 649, 126 P. 806, 1912 OK 283 (where the resignation of the county attorney by telegram was acceptable).

41 Alabama: *McMillan, Ltd v Warrior Drilling and Engineering Company, Inc.*, 512 So.2d 14 (Ala. 1986) (the name in telegram was a signature).

California: *Brewer v Horst and Lachmund Company*, 127 Cal. 643, 60 P. 418, 50 L.R.A. 240 (telegrams buying and selling hops were held sufficient for purposes of the Statute of Frauds) (1900).

Florida: *Heffernan v Keith*, Fla., 127 So.2d 903 (a telegram was signed by the telegraph company with authority of the sender) (1961); *Ashland Oil, Inc. v Pickard*, Fla., 269 So.2d 714 (a telegram constituted a signed memorandum) (1972).

Massachusetts (1972): *Providence Granite Co., Inc. v Joseph Rugo, Inc.*, Mass., 291 N.E.2d 159, 362 Mass. 888.

Michigan (1890): *Ryan v United States*, 136 U.S. 68, 10 S.Ct. 913, 34 L.Ed. 447.

Montana: *Hillstrom v Gosnay*, Mont., 614 P.2d 466 (provided the necessary intent to authenticate the signature on a telegram was shown, the typewritten signature was a proper subscription) (1980).

Nebraska: *Hansen v Hill*, 340 N.W.2d 8 (Neb. 1983), 215 Neb. 573 (a telegram accepting an offer to buy land to which the vendor's name had been affixed was considered signed under the Statute of Frauds).

New York: *Dunning & Smith v Roberts*, 35 Barb. 463 (the manipulations of a telegraph operator, upon the oral instructions of a person to send a dispatch for him, were the equivalent to a signing by that person within the Statute of Frauds) (1862); *Trevor v Wood*, 9 Tiffany 307, 36 N.Y. 307, 1867 WL 6445 (N.Y.), 3 Abb.Pr.N.S. 355, 93 Am.Dec. 511, 1 Transc.App. 248 (where dealers bought and sold bullion by exchange of telegrams, the telegrams were sufficiently signed under the Statute of Frauds) (1867).

Texas: *Adams v Abbot*, 151 Tex. 601 (1952), 254 S.W.2d 78 (a valid memorandum of contract may consist of letters and telegrams signed by the party to be charged and addressed to his agent or the other party to the contract, or even to a third person not connected with transaction).

But see Vermont: *Pike Industries, Inc. v Middlebury Associates*, 398 A.2d 280 *affirmed on other grounds* 436 A.2d 725, *cert denied*, 455 U.S. 947 (the contents of a telegram were not signed because the name of the party was not included in the body of the text) (1992).

42 162 Mo.App. 195, 144 S.W. 138.

Referee in the 1961 New York case of *La Mar Hosiery Mills, Inc. v Credit and Commodity Corporation*,[43] where he held that a name included in a telegram constituted a signature. He commented, at 190:

> It does not matter whether the telegram as delivered was copied from one written by an officer or employee of the defendant or was telephoned to the telegraph company by someone in the defendant's behalf. Precisely what happened here was not shown. The defendant could not well be heard to disclaim responsibility for the telegram and it is to the credit of the defendant that it has not attempted to do so. The telegram with the typed signature of defendant's name emanated from the defendant which is responsible for it. The signature on the telegram in suit, although typed in the office of the telegraph company, is therefore defendant's authorized signature within the requirements of the statute of frauds. In view of the way in which business is done nowadays, any other view would be unrealistic and would produce pernicious consequences, impeding the conduct of business transactions.

The 1970 case of *Yaggy v The B.V.D. Company, Inc.*[44] from North Carolina reinforced this point, where a telegram sent to the plaintiff accepting the latter's offer to purchase property was binding on the defendant. It was held that the defendant's name in print and affixed to the telegram by the same mechanical process employed by the telegraph company in reproducing other portions of the message constituted a signing within the Statute of Frauds. In the Pennsylvania case of *Hessenthaler v Farzin*,[45] it was held that a mailgram that the vendor sent to a prospective purchaser of real estate confirming acceptance of sale constituted a signed writing. After reviewing a number of cases, Hoffman J indicated, at 993, that 'We agree with these authorities that the proper, realistic approach in these cases is to look to the *reliability* of the memorandum, rather than to insist on a formal signature' (emphasis in original). He went on to say, at 994:

> The detail contained in this mailgram is such that there can be little question of its reliability. Appellants were careful to begin the mailgram by identifying themselves. They then made certain that their intention would be properly understood by declaring their acceptance, and identifying both the property and the consideration involved. In light of the primary declaration of identity, combined with the inclusion of the precise terms of the agreement, we are satisfied that the mailgram sufficiently reveals appellants' intention to adopt the writing as their own, and thus is sufficient to constitute a 'signed' writing for purposes of the Statute. Moreover, this result is consistent with the holdings of courts in other jurisdictions that have addressed the question of whether or not a telegram can be a signed writing for purposes of the Statute.

Where an agent purports to act for a principal, it was determined by the Supreme Court of California in the 1929 case of *McNear v Petroleum Export Corporation*[46] that the inclusion of the words 'Smith of Petroleum Export' at the beginning of the telegram acted as a means of identification, not authentication, and was therefore not a signature.

---

43 28 Misc.2d 764, 216 N.Y.S.2d 186.
44 70 N.C.App. 590, 173 S.E.2d 496, 72 Am.Jur.2d.
45 564 A.2d 990 (Pa.Super. 1989).
46 280 P.R.Cal. 684.

Telex

When compared to the jurisprudence developed in Europe and the United States relating to the formation of contract, Japan is less concerned for contracts to be in writing and to conform to a Statute of Frauds, but defines a contract as a judicial act to join two opposing wills.[47] As a result, the formation of a contract does not necessarily require either party to sign a contract. It is instructive to observe that the methods of communication do not appear to pose a problem in determining whether a contract has been formed in Japan. In the case of *Fawlty & Co Ltd v Matsui Shoten K.K.*,[48] the plaintiff, a New Zealand company, agreed to ship meat to Kobe port. The defendant attempted to cancel the contract and refused to accept delivery, which meant the plaintiff had to sell the meat at a loss. The contract was negotiated by a mix of letters sent by airmail and exchanges by telex. The court held that there was a contract for the purchase and sale of the meat. Although the court did not have to determine whether the communications sent and received by telex were signed by the parties, nevertheless the court must have reached the conclusion that a contract had been formed in light of the totality of the evidence, including the content of the correspondence conducted by telex. The inference is that if signatures were necessary in Japan, it is probable that a signature sent by telex will have been acceptable.

In the English case of *Clipper Maritime Ltd v Shirlstar Container Transport Ltd (The 'Anemone')*,[49] Staughton J had to determine whether a valid contract existed to perform a guarantee under the Statute of Frauds 1677. Clipper Maritime leased their vessel *Anemone* on time charter to Afram Line Ltd. Shirlstar were in the business of leasing and operating containers. By May 1983 Shirlstar was owed US$275,000 by Transaltic, an associated company to Clipper Maritime. Owners of ships became reluctant to lease their ships to such a charterer without security. The owners' brokers negotiated the charter in respect of the *Anemone* on behalf of the charterers. It was agreed at an early stage that there would be a guarantee, and the charter was eventually drawn up. The owners alleged that US$107,115.92 was due under the charter and claimed this amount from Shirlstar. Shirlstar denied they had entered into a contract of indemnity. Evidence relating to the contract between the parties was partly contained in three telexes. Staughton J determined that the context in which the telexes were exchanged demonstrated the existence of a contract, even if only implied from the circumstances by which the correspondence took place.[50] Although the point did not arise, Staughton J offered extrajudicial comments in relation to the nature of the exchange of telexes in the context of s4 of the Statute of Frauds 1677: 'I reached a provisional conclusion in the course of the argument that the answerback of the sender of a telex would constitute a signature, while that of the receiver would not since it only authenticates the document and does not convey approval of the contents'.[51]

---

47 N. Kashiwagi and E. A. Zaloom, 'Contract law and the Japanese negotiation process', in G. P. McAlinn (ed.) *The Business Guide to Japan* (Butterworth-Heinemann Asia, 1996), 89–101, republished in K. L. Port and G. P. McAlinn, *Comparative Law: Law and the Legal Process in Japan* (2nd edn, Carolina Academic Press 2003), 459.
48 Showa 33 (Wa) No.681, 10 November 1962, translated by H. Kaneko, Digital Evidence and Electronic Signature Law Review (2012) 9, 109.
49 [1987] 1 Lloyd's Rep 546, [1987] 2 WLUK 45, [1987] CLY 1846.
50 [1987] 1 Lloyd's Rep 546 at 556(b).
51 [1987] 1 Lloyd's Rep 546 at 554(b).

This conclusion followed the analysis of older cases. When a person sends a telex, it can be assumed they did so either because they intended the contents to be acted upon, or had the authority so to do. Upon receipt of the answerback, the sender may wish to revoke the original document, although to retract the document effectively may be difficult. Whether a document can be effectively revoked in this way will depend upon the circumstances of the case. When the transmission of a telex is completed, the recipient will have received the document in much the same way as if the document had been sent through the post. The recipient cannot be said to approve the content until it takes such action that demonstrates its approval. A number of issues were not examined in the judgment. Although none of these issues were in dispute in this case, they could arise in the future, as pointed out by Professor Reed:

- It does not consider the effect of the cases which appear to require a mark to be made;
- The identification messages of telex machines (and fax machines and computers) only identify the sending *machine*, not the sender;
- It is quite possible to program a telex (or a fax machine or a computer's modem) to send a false identification message; and
- If the message is stored on disk by the recipient, it is possible to edit the contents and amend the identification message to take account of the alteration.[52]

In 2003 a case relating to the Limitation Act 1980 was heard before the Court of Appeal (Civil Division), that of *Good Challenger Navegante SA v Metalexportimport SA (The 'Good Challenger')*.[53] Clarke LJ described this case as 'remarkable' because it involved an attempt by the respondent to enforce an award made by arbitrators in London against the appellant. The appellant appealed against a decision to enforce an order previously issued in 1993. In essence, there were three issues for the Court of Appeal to deal with: whether the proceedings to enforce the award were time-barred, whether there was an abuse of process and whether the award could be enforced. There were a number of matters for the court to deal with in respect of the claim that the award had become time-barred, the second of which was whether the claim was time-barred in England and Wales at the relevant time as a matter of English law under s7 of the Limitation Act 1980, which provides as follows:

> An action to enforce an award, where the submission is not under seal, shall not be brought after the expiration of six years from the date on which the cause of action accrued.

The respondents relied upon what they claimed were part payments and acknowledgements, which they said meant that the claim was not time-barred under the provisions of ss29(5) and 30 of the Limitation Act 1980. The relevant document for the purposes of the appeal was whether a telex relied upon by the appellants could be considered as an acknowledgement in writing and signed by the person making it within the meaning of s30(1). The respondent relied upon two part payments by way of authorized agents, and four acknowledgements. The validity of the award was not

---

52 Reed, 'What is a signature?', 4.1 [emphasis in original].
53 [2003] EWHC 10 (Comm), [2003] 1 Lloyd's Rep 471, [2003] 1 WLUK 69, [2003] CLY 195, appealed [2003] EWCA Civ 1668, [2004] 1 Lloyd's Rep 67, [2003] 11 WLUK 617, (2004) 101(2) LSG 27, Times, 27 November 2003, [2004] CLY 373.

challenged, but no payment was made immediately. Attempts were made to obtain payment during the following years, and the respondent relied upon two telexes, each between the respective agents of the parties, as acknowledgements of the obligation to pay the amount of the award.

At appeal, the appellant submitted that the ordinary meaning of the word 'signed' requires the maker of the document to inscribe their name or a characteristic mark on the document in their own hand, and that there is no reason to give it any other meaning in respect of s30(1) of the Limitation Act. It would follow that the section was not satisfied where a telex contained a typed signature. There was no authority on this question in the context of s30 of the Limitation Act. The content of one telex dated 17 February 1988 is set out in the judgment of Mr Michael Crane QC, sitting as a Deputy High Court Judge in the Commercial Court.[54] The telex was signed with the typewritten name 'NAVLOMAR' as authorized agent for the appellant. The question was whether the word 'NAVLOMAR' acted as a signature. The judge commented, at 61, that:

> As a matter of general principle, in my view a document is signed by the maker of it when his name or mark is attached to it in a manner which indicates, objectively, his approval of its contents. How this is done will depend upon the nature and format of the document. Thus in the case of a formal contract which prints the names of the parties and leaves a space under each name for the parties to write their names, the document will not have been signed by a party until he writes in his name in the space provided. Conversely, with a telex, where there is no such facility, the typed name of the sender at the end of the telex not only identifies the maker but leads to the inference that he has approved its contents: the typed name, therefore, constitutes his signature. Thus in my judgment each of the telexes relied on by the Claimant was signed by the sender typing in its name, or his name, at the foot of the document.

The comments by the judge reflected the previous decisions held by numerous judges over the previous three hundred years, and were approved by Clarke LJ at 22, before discussing the language used in s30 of the Limitation Act and pointing out that the language was similar to that in s4 of the Statute of Frauds 1677.[55] There was no suggestion that the name typed onto the telex was a forgery or added without authority, and Clarke LJ articulated the reasoning of the court for accepting that the signature typed onto the telex was considered a signature under s30, at 27:

> The crucial point here is that Navlomar's typed signature appeared on the telex in circumstances in which it is evident that it was put on with Navlomar's authority so that it can be seen that Navlomar (and thus the charterers) were acknowledging the debt. The purpose of the statute is to be sure that the person said to be acknowledging the debt has in truth done so. That purpose is to my mind achieved by the conclusion reached by the judge and would be thwarted were we to accede to the charterers' submissions. We were referred to a number of other authorities but, in my judgment, none of them is directly in point or affects the conclusion of the judge. I would only add that I am pleased to be able to reach this conclusion because, although telexes are not so common now, there was a time when they were the usual form of communication between chartering brokers and their principals and any other conclusion would not be commercially sensible.

54 [2003] EWHC 10 (Comm) at [55]–[57].
55 [2003] EWCA Civ 1668 at [24].

It followed that the claim was not time-barred under English law.

The acceptance of communications by telex in Australia occurred in 1985,[56] and there is a long history of recognition in the United States at the federal level.[57] Newman CJ indicated in the federal second circuit case of *Apex Oil Company v Vanguard Oil & Services Co.*[58] that the hasty formation of contracts did not pose a problem for the courts. It was held that an exchange of communications by telex satisfied the merchant's exception to the Statute of Frauds, and he indicated, at 423, that:

> Parties seeking the opportunity to make money with hurriedly arranged and briefly documented transactions ought not to expect appellate courts to provide them with extra protection against the risk that on occasion they will be held to the terms of an agreement that not every fact-finder would have found had been made.

Decisions at state level in relation to the Statue of Frauds follow this trend,[59] as exemplified in the early 1948 Californian case of *Joseph Denunzio Fruit Co. v Crane*,[60] where signatures included in messages exchanged by teletype constituted a signature. O'Connor DJ observed at 128:

> As the court understands the modus operandi of the teletype machines in modern business practice, and particularly in connection with this lawsuit, Raymond R. Crane and A. B. Rains, Jr., each had a teletype machine in his office and as the machine was operated in one office, it would type the message or memorandum simultaneously in the other office; each party was readily identifiable and known to the other by the symbols or code letters used, and there is no contention that the messages did not originate in the office of one and terminate in the office of the other. The question is just what does constitute a 'signature' or 'signing' to satisfy the Statute of Frauds in California.
>
> The court must take a realistic view of modern business practices, and can probably take judicial notice of the extensive use to which the teletype machine is being used today among business firms, particularly brokers, in the expeditious transmission of typewritten messages.

Facsimile

Documents sent by facsimile transmission have generally been accepted in common law jurisdictions.[61] The use of a facsimile transmission to send a copy of a document

---

56 *Torrac Investments Pty Ltd v Australian National Airlines Commission* [1985] ANZ Conv R 82.
57 Federal, 2nd circuit: *Interocean Shipping Company v National Shipping and Training Corporation*, 523 F.2d 527 (1975) (a signature typed into a telex under authority was sufficient to bind the principle).
58 760 F.2d 417 (1985).
59 New York: *Miller v Wells Fargo Bank International Corp.*, 406 F.Supp. 452 (1975) fn. 36, at 483 discusses the validity of a signature by way of a telex message, and raised the issue as to whether a test key on a telex is capable of being a signature.

Pennsylvania: *The Ore & Chemical Corporation v Howard Butcher Trading Corp.*, 455 F.Supp. 1150 (1978) (the exchange of telex messages between parties can constitute a written contract).

Texas: *Hideca Petroleum Corporation v Tampimex Oil International, Ltd.*, 740 S.W.2d 838 (Tex.App. – Houston [1st Dist.] 1987) (the negotiation for sale of Dubai crude oil largely by means of exchange of telex messages).

60 79 F.Supp. 117 *reversed on other grounds upon rehearing* 89 F.Supp. 962.
61 For Poland, see Case note: Poland, I KZP 29/06, Resolution of the Polish Supreme Court, commentary by A. Lach, Digital Evidence and Electronic Signature Law Review (2008) 5, 147.

to a recipient was considered in the Australian case of *Molodysky v Vema Australia Pty Ltd*,[62] where the issue was whether a facsimile transmission was considered to be service of an agreement signed by the vendor. The judge followed the test formulated in *Goodman v J Eban Limited*[63] and concluded that the vendor intended their signature on the facsimile transmission to be effective.

In the Singapore case of *Chua Sock Chen v Lau Wai Ming*[64] in relation to the service of a notice to complete a transaction, Grimberg JC held that a notice to complete was properly served when sent by means of a facsimile transmission and where the original papers were subsequently sent by post to arrive the day after transmission. The judge responded to the argument that the notice sent by facsimile transmission was not a good service for the purposes of condition 29(2) and (3) of the Singapore Law Society's Conditions of Sale 1981 at 112 B–C:

> I am unable to accept that contention. Neither of the two conditions I have quoted calls for the giving or servicing of notice to complete by a stipulated method. In these days of instantaneous communication it would be unrealistic and retrogressive, in the absence of clear words to the contrary in the conditions, to hold that the giving or service of a notice to complete under condition 29(2) and (3) by fax or telex is bad. I therefore find that the defendants' notice to complete was validly served by fax on 14 December 1988; that the period of notice began to run from 15 December.

Although the decision on the substance of the case was reversed on appeal, the members of the Court of Appeal offered no comments in relation to this aspect of the decision by Grimberg JC, which leads to the inference that his comments were adopted.

A similar issue arose in England and Wales in the case of *Re a Debtor (No 2021 of 1995), ex parte, Inland Revenue Commissioners v The Debtor; Re a Debtor (No 2022 of 1995), ex parte, Inland Revenue Commissioners v The debtor.*[65] On Friday 9 June 1995 the Commissioners of the Inland Revenue sent a completed form of proxy by first-class post with directions to the chairman of a meeting of creditors to vote against the debtors' proposals for voluntary arrangements. On the morning of the meeting, the Commissioners sent a facsimile transmission of the completed form of proxy to the chairman's office. Although not stated in the report of the case, it is probable that the form transmitted included the manuscript signature of the relevant official. When it was received, the chairman sought to verify the contents of the transmission by telephoning the Commissioners' office, but he was not able to speak to the officer handling the case. He refused to act upon the instructions sent by facsimile transmission. The original form of proxy arrived the following day. The Commissioners appealed the decision at first instance, where the district judge decided that the proxy sent by facsimile transmission was not signed as required by r8.2(3) of the Insolvency Rules 1986 SI 1986/1925. The question was whether the facsimile transmission of the

---

62 (1989) NSW ConvR 55446, [1989] AUConstrLawNlr 143; note by J. Tyrril, Australian Construction Law Newsletter, 9 (1989), 24.
63 [1954] 1 QB 550, [1954] 2 WLR 581, [1954] 1 All ER 763, [1954] 3 WLUK 22, (1954) 98 SJ 214, [1954] CLY 3173.
64 [1989] SLR 1119, the decision on the substance of the case was reversed on appeal [1992] 2 SLR 465.
65 [1996] 2 All ER 345, [1995] 11 WLUK 290, [1996] BCC 189, [1996] 1 BCLC 538, [1996] BPIR 398, [1996] CLY 3469.

form of proxy should have been accepted and acted upon by the chairman. In reaching his decision, Laddie J noted that given there was no direct authority on this point, he had to approach the issue from first principles. Having reviewed *Jenkins v Gainsford and Thring*[66] and *Goodman v J Eban Limited*,[67] he observed that:

> in the overwhelming majority of cases in which the chairman of a creditors' meeting received a proxy form, the form will bear a signature which he does not recognise and may well be illegible. Authenticity could only be enhanced if the creditor carrying suitable identification signed the form in person in the presence of the chairman. Even there the possibility of deception exists.[68]

Interestingly, he went on to suggest 'that the function of a signature is to indicate, but not necessarily prove, that the document has been considered personally by the creditor and is approved of by him'.[69] Laddie J then took the matter one stage further, and made the following observation, which is directly related to the concept of an electronic signature:

> It may be said that a qualifying proxy form consists of two ingredients. First, it contains the information required to identify the creditor and his voting instructions and, secondly, the signature performing the function set out above. When the chairman receives a proxy form bearing what purports to be a signature, he is entitled to treat it as authentic unless there are surrounding circumstances which indicate otherwise.

In reaching the conclusion that a proxy form is acceptable when sent by facsimile transmission,[70] Laddie J noted that two things happen at the same time. The contents of the form are sent, and so is the signature applied to the form, which process he described thus:

> The receiving fax is in effect instructed by the transmitting creditor to reproduce his signature on the proxy form which is itself being created at the receiving station. It follows that, in my view, the received fax is a proxy form signed by the principal or by someone authorized by him.[71]

This decision was reached in November 1995 without, it seems, the benefit of knowledge of the decision by Waller J in *Standard Bank London Ltd v Bank of Tokyo Ltd*,[72] which was delivered on 13 March 1995. The decision by Waller J is based on a tested telex between banks, which is a slightly different concept to a facsimile transmission, because a tested telex provides for a separate method of authenticating the content of the transmission. Nevertheless, in both cases emphasis was placed on the fact that a document sent by such means can be considered authentic and reliable, provided the recipient was not aware of any particulars that might indicate

---

66 (1863) 3 Sw & Tr 93, 164 ER 1208.
67 [1954] 1 QB 550, [1954] 2 WLR 581, [1954] 1 All ER 763, [1954] 3 WLUK 22, (1954) 98 SJ 214, [1954] CLY 3173.
68 [1996] 2 All ER 345, Ch D at 351 (b–c).
69 [1996] 2 All ER 345 at 351(d).
70 Laddie J indicated that the decision he made was only in relation to Part 8 of the Insolvency Rules 1986, and said: 'Different considerations may apply to faxed documents in relation to other legislation', at 352d–e.
71 [1996] 2 All ER 345, Ch D at 351(h).
72 [1995] 2 Lloyd's Rep 169, [1995] 3 WLUK 182, [1995] CLC 496, [1998] Masons CLR Rep 126, Times, 15 April 1995, [1995] CLY 397.

the document could not be trusted. A case similar to that determined by Waller J in *Standard Bank London Ltd v Bank of Tokyo Ltd* was *Industrial & Commercial Bank Ltd v Banco Ambrosiano Veneto SpA*,[73] heard before Tay Yong Kwang JC in Singapore in 2003, in which he held that a message using an authentication code sent through the SWIFT (Society for Worldwide Interbank Financial Telecommunication) system has the legal effect of binding the sender bank according to its contents, and where a recipient bank undertakes further checks on credit standing or other aspects, it does not detract from this proposition. The effect of the comments made by Laddie J, taken together with the comments by Waller J, suggest a move towards a responsibility by a recipient to consider all the circumstances of the means of authentication before acting upon the authority – although it could be argued, in accordance with established practice between banks, that a receiving bank is entirely justified in wholly relying on an instruction based exclusively on confirmation of the test code. The practical conclusion to this question is highly significant. The Bangladesh Bank is fortunate that employees in the New York Federal Reserve and an employee in an intermediary bank questioned a series of transactions authorized via the SWIFT financial transaction system in February 2016. Thieves had placed malicious software into the computer system of the central bank. They then initiated thirty-five transfers to the value of US$951m via the SWIFT financial transaction system. Five orders were executed to a value of US$101m, although a spelling error sent to an account in Sri Lanka enabled the bank to recover US$20m, resulting in an actual loss of US$81m.[74]

The Vice-Chancellor, Sir Andrew Morritt, was required to reach a decision on the identical point in *Industrial & Commercial Bank Ltd v Banco Ambrosiano Veneto SpA* in the case of *PNC Telecom plc v Thomas*,[75] as to whether the service of a notice sent by facsimile transmission for an extraordinary general meeting on a members' requisition under s368 of the Companies Act 1985 was valid. By s368, notice to call a meeting is required to be deposited at the registered office of the company. The claimant argued that the notice was not valid on three counts: because it was sent by facsimile transmission, and the use of a facsimile transmission was not permitted within the meaning of 'deposited' in s368; that the Companies Act 1985 (Electronic Communication) Order 2000 (SI 2000/3373) had made service by electronic means valid in respect of some sections of the 1985 Act, but not for s368; and there was a requirement to know that the notice received at the registered office was genuine, which meant that it was not permissible to send a notice by facsimile transmission. Sir Andrew referred to a number of authorities in which a facsimile transmission had been accepted by the courts, and rejected all of the arguments put forward by the claimant. He considered that the deposit of the notice by facsimile transmission was valid, and robustly responded, at 94 a–b, to the illogical claim about the reliability of such a means of transmitting a document thus:

> For the reasons given by Laddie J in the last citation, there is nothing inherent in a fax transmission to make it more or less reliable than the post. It is true that a fax may be falsified by a cut and paste operation but forgery and falsification is equally possible, usually by other means, in connection with postal and personal transmission too.

73 [2003] 1 SLR 221.
74 https://en.wikipedia.org/wiki/Bangladesh_Bank_robbery.
75 [2002] EWHC 2848 (Ch), [2002] 12 WLUK 537, [2003] BCC 202, [2004] BCLC 88, [2003] CLY 532.

The same position with respect to facsimile transmissions holds in Canada, where, in the case of *Re United Canso Oil & Gas Ltd*,⁷⁶ proxy forms submitted with a facsimile or mechanically rendered signature were held to be sufficient. Hallett J at 289 paragraph 17 made the following point:

> Today's business could not be conducted if stamped signatures were not recognized as legally binding. The affixing of a stamp conveys the intention to be bound by the document so executed just as effectively as the manual writing of a signature by hand. I would point out that no one questions the validity of millions of payroll cheques signed by facsimile signatures.

This view is echoed in the Singapore decision of Lim Teong Qwee JC in the case of *Masa-Katsu Japanese Restaurant Pte Ltd v Amara Hotel Properties Pte Ltd*,⁷⁷ in which he held that a facsimile transmission of a request to extend the term of a lease was a valid form of communicating. He commented, at 18:

> The written request dated 4 October 1997 was in fact received by the landlord. It was received by fax on 10 October 1997. It was not suggested that it was received other than at the landlord's office where it could be attended to immediately. It was undoubtedly in writing when it was received. Communication by fax is not uncommon. It is fast. It is efficient. It accords with the practice of the business community. It seems to me that where as in this case a written request is to be made it is sufficiently made as much where the request is written on paper that is physically transported to the office of the person to whom the request is made as where it is transmitted by fax and received in written form at that person's office.

Consideration was also given to a signature sent by way of facsimile transmission in the German case of GmSOGB 1/98 before the Gemeinsamer Senat der obersten Gerichtshöfe des Bundes (Joint Senate of the Federal High Courts) in 2000. In this instance, the court had to decide whether or not a facsimile transmission sent directly from a computer (Computerfax) with a scanned manuscript signature complied with the requirements of written form for formal court pleadings. In the normal course of events, various rules of German procedural law require formal court pleadings to be signed with a manuscript signature, and a number of Federal High Courts have reached decisions on this point.⁷⁸ The court held that it was sufficient to transfer pleadings electronically in this manner, providing the documents were signed with a scanned manuscript signature, or if the document transmitted indicated that the document could not be signed personally because of the method of transmission. The members of the court reached this conclusion on the basis that the formal requirements of procedural law do not serve as an end in themselves, and the purpose of requiring court proceedings to be in written form is to identify the sender and ensure the document was sent with the sender's knowledge and intent. As a result, the intention of the sender was not seriously in doubt because of the method of transmission.⁷⁹ Similar decisions were made in Hungary⁸⁰ and Lithuania,⁸¹ in which the Supreme Administrative Court in its ruling of 13 April 2006 held that the copy of an administrative decision sent by

---

76 (1980) 12 BLR 130, 76 APR 282, 41 NSR (2d) 282 (TD).
77 [1999] 2 SLR 332.
78 Federal Social Court, Beschluß vom 15.10.1996 – 14 BEg 9/96; Federal Administrative Court, Beschluß vom 19.12.1994 – 5 B 79/94.
79 M. Knopp, case note, Digital Evidence and Electronic Signature Law Review (2005) 2, 103.
80 Case number BDT 2001/496.
81 *UAB 'Bite Lietuva' v Communications Regulatory Authority* AS14-77-06.

facsimile transmission constituted a proper form of notification by the governmental institution of its decision.

In the United States, a federal court on the ninth circuit found itself severely constrained by a set of extremely strict rules laid down by the Bureau of Land Management in the case of *Gilmore v Lujan*[82] respecting documents sent by facsimile transmission. In this instance, an application was sent by facsimile transmission because the original postal application had not arrived on time. The Bureau refused to accept the documents sent by facsimile transmission because the papers were not signed with a manuscript signature. Upon appeal, this decision was upheld because the signature was required to be a manuscript signature only, and no other form was permitted. The Bureau of Land Management required applications to be holographically signed in ink by each potential lessee, and machine or rubber-stamped signatures were not acceptable. The rule was altered after the case of *W. H. Gilmore*,[83] where Gilmore protested the lease was awarded to an applicant that used a rubber stamp as a signature. The regulations were deliberately altered to permit only manuscript signatures thereafter. Although the regulations required the signature to be in ink, nevertheless the Board determined, in the later case of *Jack Williams*,[84] that a signature signed with a lead pencil was adequate. Nelson CJ criticized the decision, indicating, at 142, that:

> Justice Holmes observed that citizens dealing with their government must turn square corners ... Gilmore turned all but the last millimetre, but that millimetre, whose traverse is jealously guarded by the BLM, was his undoing. Relief to Gilmore in this narrow case would expose BLM to no fraud or risk of fraud, as his bona fides are beyond question. If Gilmore and those other few luckless applicants whose documents are stored rather than delivered by the Postal Service are to get any relief, it must come at the hands of the BLM. As shown by this case, those hands are more iron than velvet. We can only suggest to BLM that the body politic would not be put at risk by the granting of relief in these narrow and rare situations.

The use of facsimile transmissions has been challenged in other situations, such as arbitration[85] and elections,[86] although in *Bogue v Sizemore*[87] there was no dispute about a contract disseminated by facsimile. In addition, cases have occurred under the Statute of Frauds,[88] although not always successfully.

---

82 947 F.2d 1409 (9th Cir. 1991).
83 41 IBLA 25 (1979).
84 91 IBLA 355 (1986).
85 New York: *In the Matter of American Multimedia, Inc. v Dalton Packaging, Inc.*, 143 Misc.2d 295, 540 N.Y.S.2d 410 (an order was transmitted by facsimile machine that only contained the first of two pages of an order form, stating that all orders were subject to the terms and conditions on the reverse of the form, which was not sent. It was held that the terms did apply, because the petitioner had filed over 100 such orders in the previous three years) (1989).
86 New Jersey: *Madden v Hegadorn*, 565 A.2d 725 (N.J.Super.L. 1989), 236 N.J.Super. 280, *affirmed* 571 A.2d 296 (N.J. 1989), 239 N.J.Super. 268 (a document sent by facsimile transmission containing a manuscript signature was deemed effective for filing a nomination petition, and any technical defects were cured when the candidate filed the original documents the day after the facsimile transmission was sent).
87 241 Ill.App.3d 250, 608 N.E.2d 1246 (Ill.App.4th Dist. 1993).
88 New York: *WPP Group USA, Inc. v The Interpublic Group of Companies, Inc.*, 644 N.Y.S.2d 205, 228 A.D.2d 296 (it was premature to decide whether the Statute of Frauds was satisfied where an unsigned facsimile transmission on the letterhead of the sender was sent) (1996). For the merchant's exception

In Canada, forms of proxy sent by facsimile transmission were the subject matter of the British Columbia case of *Beatty v First Exploration Fund 1987 and Company, Limited Partnership*.[89] In this case, it was held that forms of proxy sent by facsimile transmission were sufficient to meet the signature requirements under a limited partnership agreement. Hinds J indicated, at 383, that 'The faxed proxies were not themselves signed, but they bore the photographic reproduction of the original of the limited partner who executed the particular proxy'. He went on to say, at 383, that 'The law has endeavoured to take cognizance of, and to be receptive to, technological advances in the means of communication. The development of that approach may be observed in a number of cases, including the following.' At 385 he addressed the argument relating to the theoretical possibility that such transmissions might be the subject of fraud, which is hardly an argument to use when the authenticity of the document in question has not been challenged:

> It was argued by counsel for the Fund that validating faxed proxies would increase the risk of fraud, create uncertainty, and give an unfair advantage to those limited partners who had access to a telecopier or fax machine. I reject that argument. Faxed proxies are, in effect, a photocopy of an original copy. They reveal what is depicted on an original copy, including an exact replica of the signature of the person who signed the original proxy. I observe no greater opportunity for the perpetration of a fraud by the use of faxed copies than by the use of original copies. The same observation applies to the matter of uncertainty.

---

see the New York case of *Bazak International Corp. v Mast Industries, Inc.*, 140 Ad.2d 211, 528 N.Y.S.2d 62, 6 UCC Rep.Serv.2d 375, *appeal granted by* 72 N.Y.2D 808, 529 N.E.2d 425, 533 N.E.2d 57 (N.Y. 1988), *Order reversed by* 73 N.Y.2D 113, 535 N.E.2d 633, 538 N.Y.2d 503, 57 USLW 2520, 82 A.L.R.4th 689, 7 UCC Rep.Serv.2d 1380 (N.Y. 1989) where annotated telecopies ('telecopies' is a trademark sometimes used for a facsimile machine) of headed purchase order forms signed by the alleged purchaser and sent to the alleged seller and retained without objection came within the merchant's exception to the Statute of Frauds.
89   25 BCLR2d 377 (1988).

8
The writing material

In the days before the development of techniques to identify microscopic indentations or traces of lead on paper, the material used to write on a document could cause conceptual problems. The nature of the writing material used to affix a signature was raised in the case of *Geary v Physic*.[1] An objection was taken where a promissory note was signed using a pencil. At the trial, the Lord Chief Justice, Abbott CJ, thought the promissory note was sufficiently indorsed, and directed the members of the jury to find a verdict for the plaintiff. He also permitted the plaintiff to challenge this finding. The matter was subsequently argued before Abbott CJ, and Bayley and Holroyd JJ. In his judgment, the Lord Chief Justice pointed out: 'There is no authority for saying that where the law requires a contract to be in writing, that writing must be in ink'.[2] This decision was made before the development of the forensic analysis of materials and the use of technology as a means of detecting changes to materials. Although it is now possible to detect the erasure of a manuscript signature if it were to be affixed using a pencil, the principle established by this decision remains sound. The rationale for this decision is the principle that a signature was affixed to the document with an intent that it should be acted upon. Hence the type of writing material used is irrelevant, providing it is not removed from the document. This decision may also be considered correct on the premise that the promissory note was only valid for a limited period of time, and the use of a pencil to sign the note may not have been considered relevant because there was no requirement to retain a permanent record of the note.[3]

In *Bateman v Pennington*,[4] the testator died suddenly, and in his effects two testamentary papers were discovered. The first paper was written in ink, and the date and signature of the testator inserted in pencil, preceded with the words 'in case of accident I sign this my will', also in pencil. The second paper was not dated, but subscribed by the testator in ink. Witnesses subscribed neither paper. On appeal to the Judicial Committee of the Privy Council, Lord Brougham, providing judgment, reversed the court below. The words in pencil could be construed as deliberative, but taking into account all the circumstances of the case, it was determined that the testator intended to die testate, and the appellant was entitled to probate.

In *Lucas v James*,[5] a series of remarks on a draft under-lease were written in pencil, including the words 'I agree to these terms, subject to the above observations. W. M. James'. In this instance, the plaintiff sought specific performance, while the defendant denied an agreement had been reached, arguing in part that the comments made by

---

1 (1826) 5 B & C 234, 108 ER 87.
2 (1826) 5 B & C 234 at 237.
3 For a case on the use of a ballpoint pen, see J. Bing and J. Hvarre, 'Case note Denmark: U 1959.40/1H' (2009) 6 Digital Evidence and Electronic Signature Law Review, 277.
4 (1840) 3 MooPCC 223.
5 (1849) 7 Hare 410, 68 ER 170.

him on the draft, being made in pencil, were not intended to be binding. Although the claim failed for other reasons, Sir James Wigram VC made the extrajudicial remark that these words, taken in conjunction with a previous comment made by the defendant on the same draft, would, on the face of it, bind him to the terms of the under-lease.[6] The Vice-Chancellor considered that the remarks made in pencil demonstrated a willingness to be bound by the amended document. In this instance, the use of pencil on the document was deemed perfectly acceptable as evidence of the writer's intent to agree the terms of the document.

Whether the nature of a document had been changed sufficiently as the result of alterations made in pencil was the subject of *In the Goods of Adams*[7] and *Co-operative Bank plc v Tipper*.[8] In *Adams*, the deceased executed a printed form will. Additions were made in pencil and ink. Some of the writing in pencil had been partly rubbed out, and some had been written over in ink. Lord Penzance concluded that the intention of the deceased was for the additions made in ink to supersede the writing in pencil, and the words in pencil were excluded from probate.

In *Co-operative Bank plc v Tipper*, Mr and Mrs Tipper entered into a personal guarantee with the bank, but it transpired that the document erroneously described the defendants personally as both the customer (i.e. the principal debtor) and the guarantor. The bank applied to the court to rectify the error after Mr and Mrs Tipper's company went into liquidation. Mr and Mrs Tipper opposed the application of the bank on the basis that where a document is altered in a material way, it becomes void, and therefore unenforceable. In this instance, a person unknown working for the bank used a pencil to strike out the names of Mr and Mrs Tipper and add the name and address of the company. Cooke J concluded that the proper evidential inference to draw was that the alterations constituted a drafting amendment. The changes made in pencil were not intended to alter the substance of the document, but were meant to propose that the names be put in the correct place in the document. As a result, the use of pencil did not alter the content of the document because the use of a pencil constituted a series of suggestions to correct errors in the document.

In a case from Scotland, *Jollie v Lennie*,[9] the testator wrote a purported will by hand in pencil on each side of a single sheet of A5 paper. The testator signed the will before a witness, who also signed. Both signatures were in pencil. The will was held to be effective.

The use of a lead pencil has also been the subject of a number of decisions in the United States of America, including bills of exchange,[10] the Statute of Frauds,[11]

---

6 (1849) 7 Hare 410 at 419.
7 *In the Goods of Adams* (1872) LR 2 P & D 367.
8 [1996] 4 All ER 366, [1995] 11 WLUK 74, Times, 5 July 1996, [1996] CLY 409.
9 [2014] ScotCS CSOH_45.
10 New York: *Brown v The Butchers & Drovers' Bank*, 6 Hill 443, 41 Am.Dec. 755 (the endorsement of a bill of exchange using a lead pencil was sufficient) (1844).

Vermont: *Clossen v Stearns*, 4 Vt. 11, 1831 WL 2104 (Vt.), 23 Am.Dec. 245 (the endorsement of a promissory note by means of a lead pencil was held to be valid) (1831).

11 Missouri: *Great Western Printing Co. v Belcher*, 127 Mo.App. 133, 104 S.W. 894 (the words 'Guaranteed. Belcher' written in lead pencil across the face of the original account was a signature, even though the signature did not include a first name) (1907).

wills[12] and deeds, as in the 1920 Missouri case of *Kleine v Kleine*,[13] in which John Kleine granted his sister a lease on a portion of land, and he signed it with a lead pencil. It was held to be a valid instrument. Graves J indicated, at 610, what he thought of Kleine and his motive for using a lead pencil in this instance:

> Kleine's testimony in the case tends to leave a bad taste in the judicial mouth. Among other things, he requested that the lease be signed with a lead pencil, and says that he 'figured' that it was no good when he signed it, 'because there was no starting point'. All this was after the sister had put her money into the improvements.

The judge went on, at 611, to observe that:

> The real issue in the case is not the views expressed by John Kleine, to the effect that he signed the lease (in lead pencil, at his own suggestion) because he thought it invalid, owing to the absence of a starting point. He seems not only to have had that idea, but the other erroneous view, entertained by many laymen, that a deed must be signed with a pen and ink.

His comments illustrate the frustration felt by many lawyers resulting from the erroneous and endlessly inaccurate comments made by lay people in respect of legal issues.

However, it is the use of a lead pencil on a judicial document in 1823 that serves to illustrate the fallacy about the invalid use of lead pencil as a means of affixing a signature to a document, and also in relation to whether a document is open to attack. In the Columbia case of *United States v Thompson*,[14] it was held that an indictment for assault and battery for violently beating a slave signed by a justice of the peace with a lead pencil did not contain a sufficient signature. The reason given by Cranch CJ was that 'it is liable to be so easily obliterated'. This is a false conclusion based on an erroneous premise. The logic of the reasoning runs as follows: a material that can be erased was used to affix the signature to the document, ergo the signature is not valid because it is possible to erase the signature. It is correct that the material impressed onto paper by a lead pencil can be erased, but the possibility that the writing can be erased does not prevent the document from having been signed. In this instance, the document was signed with the manuscript signature of a justice of the peace. The evidence of the signature was clear for all to see, which meant the signature was sufficient. Had the signature been erased, then the integrity of the document would have been questioned, and, depending on the strength or weakness of the evidence tendered and tested before the court, a decision could be made as to the authenticity of the document, which in turn would enable the trier of fact to determine whether the document had been signed or not.

New York: *Merritt v Clason*, 12 Johns. 102, 7 Am.Dec. 286, 12 N.Y.S.C. 1814–15 92 *affirmed as The Executors of Clason v Bailey*, 14 Johns. 484 (where a memorandum of a contract was written down in a notebook using a lead pencil, the document was a sufficient memorandum within the Statute of Frauds) (1817).

South Carolina: *Draper v Pattina*, 29 S.C.L. 292, 2 Speers 292, 1844 WL 2584 (S.C.App.L.) (a memorandum written using a lead pencil was not a valid objection) (1844).

12 Pennsylvania: *Appeal of Knox*, 131 P. 220, 18 A. 1021, 6 L.R.A. 353, 17 Am.St.Rep. 798 (an instrument written in lead pencil was sufficient to be admitted as a will) (1890).
13 219 S.W. 610, 281 Mo. 317.
14 2 Cranch C.C. 409, 28 F.Cas. 89, 2 D.C. 409, No 16484 (1823).

Lawyers often use this argument relating to documents in electronic and digital form. The argument runs like this: because it is possible to forge an email, facsimile transmission or electronic signature (any form of electronic signature), ergo the email, facsimile transmission or electronic signature should not be admitted because of the possibility of forgery. Astonishingly, this argument was successfully used in the German case of *AG Bonn Urteil vom 25.10.2001 3 C 193/01 Beweiskraft von E-Mails, JurPC Web-Dok. 332/2002*, where the claimant sued the defendant for a broker's fee for acting as an intermediary for the sale of cigarettes. The claim was dismissed on the basis that there was no sufficient proof, because the emails submitted in evidence had no value as evidence, because it is generally known that emails can be easily altered or forged. This argument is also fallacious. Any paper document can be forged, such as a letter from a commercial entity or a government, and lawyers are required to sift through documentary evidence regularly to test the authenticity of documents. The forgery of evidence is hardly new, and if this argument were to be accepted by judges, which it seems to be in some cases, then by logical extension, any item of documentary evidence could be excluded because it was possible to forge it. If it is suggested that an item of evidence has been forged, the question should be raised before trial, so that the party relying on the evidence has the opportunity to adduce evidence to prove the document is genuine. Unsound arguments based on a flawed foundation have no place in a court.

9

An incorrect signature and absence of a signature

Unusually, the Scottish Court of Session had to decide whether an incorrect signature was sufficient in the case of *Williamson v Williamson*.[1] In this case, the issue was whether one of the witnesses, Mr David Carment Reid Wilson, a solicitor, failed to subscribe his name or signature as a witness on the will of the late Mrs Rachel Macintosh Macrae Williamson dated 11 April 1988. The solicitor wrote the name 'D C R Williamson'. The defenders urged the court to accept the signature as valid. In delivering the opinion of the court, Lord Marnoch discussed the authorities, but indicated that, when considered objectively, it was clear that Mr Wilson had failed to adhibit his normal or customary signature, or any customary equivalent to his signature, on the occasion in question.

Three further illustrations demonstrate the willingness of judges to imply a document has been signed in the absence of a manuscript signature. In the case of *Rist v Hobson*,[2] an agreement for the sale and purchase of an estate had been drawn up but not signed by either party. The vendor sought an order for specific performance, and Sir John Leach VC reached the conclusion that where the agreement was in writing, it would be presumed the document was signed unless evidence to the contrary was adduced to rebut the presumption. It is not clear from the report whether the agreement had been committed to writing by either of the parties in this instance. In the later case of *Bleakley v Smith*,[3] the agreement had been written in the hand of one of the parties. Mr Bridges agreed to sell five houses in Liverpool to John Bleakley. The only evidence to this agreement was a memorandum, written by Mr Bridges: 'July 26th, 1839. John Bleakley agrees with J R Bridges to take the property in Cable Street for the net sum of £248 10s'. Mr Bridges died on 10 February 1840, but had not conveyed the property. In an action against Mr Bridges' executors, the Vice-Chancellor made a declaration that the memorandum was a valid and binding contract and ordered specific performance and execution of a conveyance of the properties. The Vice-Chancellor merely stated that the agreement was sufficiently signed to take it out of the Statute of Frauds. In all probability, the reason for so finding was partly because the memorandum was drawn up in the hand of Mr Bridges and he had received the purchase price. In such circumstances, there was sufficient evidence to show he intended to sell the properties. It appears that the obligation was considered to be 'entire', thus permitting an order for specific performance.

In the 1910 Massachusetts case of *Meads v Earle*,[4] the testatrix, Sarah J. Armstrong, was shortly to sail for Italy. She was described as an 'intelligent, self-reliant woman'. She wrote her own will without assistance on a blank wills form. Although she obtained signatures of the requisite number of witnesses, she failed to sign the will at the end

---

1 1997 SC 94, 1997 SLT 1044, [1997] ScotCS CSIH 3, 1997 GWD 9398, 1997 SCLR 561.
2 (1824) 1 Sim & St 543, 57 ER 215.
3 (1840) 11 Sim 149, 59 ER 831.
4 205 Mass. 553, 91 N.E. 916, 29 L.R.A.N.S. 63 (1910).

of the document. The judge at first instance and the members of the Supreme Court of Massachusetts concluded that the will had been signed, because she wrote the entire document in her own hand. In giving the judgment of the appellate court, Hammond J acknowledged, at 918, that the case law was 'not in complete harmony', and listed the relevant cases. It appears that the judges, in reaching their decision, were impressed with the evidence of her being strong-minded and self-reliant.

These cases illustrate that, despite failing to comply with formal requirements, the content of a document can be authenticated where there is sufficient evidence to show the person signing the document adopted the content.

Index

abbreviation of name as signature
   35 fn 112, 37
absence of
   full signature 28
   signature 66 fn 7, 89
administrative use 58
arthritis 54 fn 69
assisted signature 24
ataxia 53
attorney, power of, cablegram 71 fn 3
Australia
   facsimile 78
   forged manuscript signature 11 fn 1
   name typed on document, adopt
      65 fn 4
   telex 78
authenticated signature fiction 67
authentication
   chirograph 17
   court records 16
   differing assertions as to 2
   distinctive handwriting 16
   methods of, before manuscript
      signatures 15
   objects 15
   scribes 16
   seal 15
   sign of cross 17
   signature as means of 4, 9
   SWIFT 81
   witnesses 9
authority, signature and
   agent 46
   attorney 65
   initials, as agent 27, 31 fn 83
   rubber stamp 53
   signature machines 64
   telegraph 71, 72, 73 fn 41
   telex 76, 79 fn 57
   typewritten name 65

Barclay Street, New York 34
bill of costs
   abbreviation of name 37
   signed with rubber stamp 56
bill of exchange
   numbers as substitute for name
      21 fn 16
   signed by mark 19
   using lead pencil 86 fn 10

Canada
   facsimile transmission 82, 84
   illegible signature 23
   initials as signature, will 30
   rubber stamp 53, 55, 58
   typed signature 69
   unknown method of signature 12,
      58 fn 88
carrier
   document 6
   durable record 10
   paper, physical alteration of 12
cheque
   generally 2
   initials 31 fn 82
   name printed 3, 13
cipher (tuğra) of the Ottoman sultans
   4 fn 18
court record, seal imprint 43
cross, sign of 17

deeds 21, 23, 26, 33, 42, 63, 87
definition 4, 6
   contentious expansion of meaning 32
document
   intention to authenticate and
      adopt 13

ecclesiastical use, rubber stamp 56
Edward III 19

electronic signature, first form 70
erf 20
erysipelas 65
evidence
    burden, evidential 11, 12
    burden of proof 51, 65
    electronic documents, false arguments 88
    unable to determine type of signature 58 fn 88

facsimile 49 fn 50 and 52, 62, 63
    generally 78
    Interpretation Act 6
    rubber stamp 54, 55, 56, 58, 59, 60 fn 99 and 100 and 101 and 102 and 104, 62, 62 fn 104
fingerprint 21, 44
functions of signature *see* Chapter 2
    cautionary function 9
    channelling function 10
    primary evidential function 9
    protective function 9
    record keeping function 10
    secondary evidential function 9

guarantee
    correction of error 86
    initials, property 30
    lease signed by signature machine 64
    Statute of Frauds 1677, telex 75
guiding hand 25

handwriting
    analysis of manuscript signature 12
    establish authenticity 16

identifying phrase, signature 36
illegible writing 22
impression of mark as signature
    lithographed name 52
    printed name 44
    rubber stamp 52
    seal imprint 15, 39
    signature machines 64
    stencil-pen 62
initials as signature 24, 27

Human Fertilisation and Embryology Act 1990 30
indecipherable marks 24
    judicial use 28
    rights in property 30
    Statute of Frauds 1677 27
    United States of America 31
    voting 30
    wills *see* wills
intention
    authenticate and adopt 5, 13, 37
    stamp 58, 8
insurance document
    mark, use of 21 fn 18

judicial use of signature
    initials 28
    pencil *see* pencil
    mark as signature, notice of appeal 49 fn 54
    rubber stamp 54, 61
    seal imprint, record 43
    telegrams 73 fn 40

lease
    autopen 64
    facsimile 82
    initials 30, 31 fn 83
    name acts to authenticate 48
    pencil *see* pencil
    rubber stamp 83
    seal 42
    typed that did not bind 66 fn 6
Limitation Act 1980, telex 76
lithographed name, as signature 52

malicious software 81
manuscript signature
    defences 11
    disputing 11
    early example of 19
    functions of *see* function of signature
    handwriting analysis of 12
    identity of person affixing 12
    intent to authenticate and adopt 13
    writing material used for 85

Index

mark
    assisted mark 24
    bills of exchange 19
    cross 17
    generally 39
    interests in real property 40
    promissory note 20 fn 6
    United States of America 21
    wills *see* wills
mechanical marks
    facsimile 78
    introduction 64
    telegram 70
    telex 75
    typewriting 64
mistake as to name 25

name
    abbreviation of 37
    fictitious 26
    lithographed name 52
    mistake as to name 25
    printed name 44
    promissory note, name of another 26
    surname 32
    trade name 33
    variation of 26
    without signature 25
    without permission 26
    words other than 35
National Heritage Centre for Horseracing & Sporting Art, Newmarket 39
New Zealand
    authenticated signature fiction 67, 68
    initials 30
    telex, Japanese proceedings 75
    see also wills
notary 11, 20, 60 fn 101
numbers, substitute for name 21 fn 16

object, as authentication 15

partial signature 34
pencil
    alterations 86
    indecipherable marks 24
    indictment 87
    lease 87
    promissory note 85
    signature 26 fn 49, 83
    Statute of Frauds 87 fn 11
    Notice of objection 54
    under lease 86
    United States of America 86
    will *see* wills
pictogram signature 19 fn 2
power of attorney 71 fn 32
printed name
    signature 44
    United States of America 49
professional firm, abbreviated name 37
promissory note
    forgery, acknowledge as own 50
    mark 20 fn 6, 21 fn 16
    pencil *see* pencil
    printed name 50
    rubber stamp 60 fn 99
    surname 32
    use of name of another 26
protective function *see* functions of signature

record
    chirograph 17
    function *see* functions of signature
    tally stick 17 fn 13
regularity, presumption of 12, 23
rights in property 30
rubber stamp
    administrative use 58
    ballots, signing by rubber stamp 29, 57, 60 fn 98
    ecclesiastical use 56
    enforcement notices 59
    information, an 58
    judicial use 54
    as signature 11, 50, 52
    Solicitors Act 1932 56
    Statute of Frauds 55
    United States of America 59
    voting 54
    wills 53

Scotland
    Christian name 26
    deeds 33
    familiar name 36
    identifying phrase, use of 36
    illegible signature 23
    incorrect signature 89
    initials 29, 30
    mark signing by 34
    partial signature 34
    pencil *see* pencil
    property, rights 30 fn 78
    surname 33
    stamp, will 53
    stencil-pen 62
    stopped writing, whether signature effective 34
    surname as signature, deed 33
    variation of name to sign will 26
scribe, as document authentication method 16
seal imprint 15, 40
    authentication 2, 15
    court records 43
    distrust 40
    forgery 16 fn 4, 39
    historical use of 15
    holiday seal 44
    Japanese seal, recognition 44
    legal charge 42
    real property 40
    wills *see* wills
Shepperton's Code 22 fn 21
sign of the cross 17
signature
    absence of 89
    assisted signature 24
    authentication 4, 9
    authenticated signature fiction 67
    authority *see* authority, signature and
    chirograph 17
    definitions 4, 6
    disputing *see* Chapter 3
    false signature, painting 5 fn 21
    form and function 3
    functions *see* functions of signature
    identifying phrase 36
    identity 5

illegible 4, 6, 22, 80
judicial approach to defining 1, 19, 23, 32, 58, 65, 77
machines 64
manuscript *see* manuscript signature
objects 15
odd position 31
painting 2
partial signature 26, 34
purpose of 1
stencil-pen 62
surname 32
third person 33
validity, judicial consideration 3
Singapore
    facsimile 79, 81, 82
Society for Worldwide Interbank Financial Telecommunication (SWIFT)
    authentication code 81
Solicitors Act 1932
    abbreviated name 37
    rubber stamp 56
South Africa
    assisted signature or mark 24
    cheque, name printed 3
    erf 20
    headed notepaper 24
    indecipherable writing 24
    initials 30
    mark 20
    pencil *see* pencil
    promissory note, mark 20 fn 6
    telegram 73 fn 36
    thumb prints 44
stamp, engraving 53
Statute of Frauds 1677
    absence of signature 89
    identifying phrase 36
    initials 28
    name without signature 25
    printed name 44
    rubber stamp 52
    seal imprint 15
    surname 32
    telegram 70
    telex 75
    typed signature 64

Index

stencil-pen 62
surname 32
    contentious expansion 32
    deeds 33
    not signature 28 fn 59
    signature 22, 27 fn 52, 29, 30
    Statute of Frauds 32

tally stick 17 fn 13
telegram 70
    evidential foundation 72
    United States of America 72
telex 75
tested telex 80
totemic signature 19 fn 2
thumb print 44 fn 26
trade name 33
Tudor, Mary 52
tuğra 4 fn 18
typed signature 64

under-lease, pencil remarks written in 90

voting
    initials 30
    printed name 51 fn 61
    rubber stamp 54
    surname 30
    variation of name 26

wills
    assisted or guiding signature or mark 25
    Christian name 26
    cross 25 fn 41
    familiar name 36
    guiding hand 25
    illegible writing 23
    incorrect signature 89
    infirmity 35
    initials 29, 30
    mark 19
    mistake as to name 25
    partial signature 34
    pencil *see* pencil
    seal imprint 15, 39
    signature not intended to be signor's signature 13
    stamp, engraving 53
    tripartite chirographs 18
    undecipherable scrawl 23
    variation of name 26
    words other than name 35
    written in own hand, not signed 90
witness and scribes 16
words other than name 35
writing material *see* Chapter 8

your loving mother 35, 36
your miserable father 27

www.ingramcontent.com/pod-product-compliance
Ingram Content Group UK Ltd.
Pitfield, Milton Keynes, MK11 3LW, UK
UKHW060455150426
5217IPUK00027B/2079